GRACE
that
SAVES

*Embracing the Truth of God's
Unmerited Favor*

JAY R. LEACH

Order this book online at www.trafford.com
or email orders@trafford.com

Most Trafford titles are also available at major online book retailers.

Printed in the United States of America.

ISBN: 978-1-4907-2411-9 (sc)
ISBN: 978-1-4907-2412-6 (e)

Library of Congress Control Number: 2014900831

Trafford rev. 01/16/2014

 www.trafford.com

North America & international
toll-free: 1 888 232 4444 (USA & Canada)
fax: 812 355 4082

CONTENTS

DEDICATION

I dedicate this book to our Lord and Savior, Jesus Christ and for His service. I trust it will be used in His hands as an instrument to help prepare the Bride for His soon return. I thank Him for those He has brought into my life who have exemplified to me His grace that saves.

- My wife, Magdalene, who has shown me *great grace*. **Who can find a virtuous woman? . . . . The heart of her husband doth safely trust in her . . . .** (Proverbs 31:10, 11). The peace my heart has in trusting my wife has allowed me to understand the grace that comes in trusting our Lord.

- To the Apostles, Prophets, Evangelists, Pastors, and Teachers of the Bread of Life Ministries comprising: The Bread of Life Christian Center and Church, The Bread of Life Bible Institute [1 School in 8 Locations], and the Bread of Life Church and Ministries Fellowship. Your constant encouragement and support continually remind Magdalene and me of the depths of sacrifice and commitment involved in being faithful to those people God has put within our reach.

- To my fellow followers of Jesus Christ who have entered into the mystery and joys of the Bread of Life Church, I want to thank you for seeing and joining the vision with us as we continue to define what it means to follow Christ in authentic Christian Community. Thank you for allowing us time to share these concepts with the broader body of Christ—not only to teach and write about them, but more importantly—to live them!

INTRODUCTION

It has often been expressed that the primary leadership of the Reformation [Restoration] did not go far enough in their restoration of the New Testament Church. Martin Luther got it right on how we are saved [justification]. *"The just shall live by faith"* (Galatians 3:11), was one of the revelatory truths of God's Word that rallied the Reformers. We praise God for the reformer John Wycliffe who believed that the people should be able to read the Bible in their own language; and by the grace of God he worked hard to get the truth of God's Word into the hearts of the masses. That is an on-going mission which must be repeated in each new generation.

Notice, a half century after the Reformation began the church was in crisis, because it misunderstood that justification or salvation is of God through **grace alone**—believers coming out of the Medieval or Dark Ages were taught that sanctification [spiritual maturity] was accomplished through works of the flesh. They were constantly reminded how much their relationship with God depended on their works. The sad news is many local churches continue to practice this pre-Reformation church model of ministry to this day.

This theological error has come full circle today. The results of it is witnessed in every city, town and village of America were citizens no longer believe God is relevant, that He no longer loves and cares, that He created the world and left it to feign for itself. Add to that the many local churches that rely upon legalism and performance in the flesh, rather than upon God's grace *alone* through the power of the indwelling Holy Spirit. He leads, guides, and teaches the *restored* truths of the Gospel of Grace. Teachers were raised up during the Reformation *to help Christians know what they believed and why they believed it.* Today, God is meeting that need by raising up desperately needed teachers for that very purpose.

The Bread of Life Bible Institute and thousands of Para ministries across America and around the world are established and Spirit-led for "such a time as this." Magdalene and I were led of the Spirit to establish the Bread of Life Bible Institute fifteen years ago specifically to equip the saints for that purpose. If the churches would return to their Christ-given mission, biblical world view and teaching ministries, millions would be added to the churches.

The apostle Paul encountered the same insidious error and addressed the problem in Galatians 3:1-3:

*You foolish Galatians, who has bewitched you that you should not obey the truth, before whose eyes Jesus Christ was clearly portrayed among you as crucified? This only I want to learn from you: Did you receive the Spirit by the **works of the law,** or by the **hearing of faith?** Are you so foolish? **Having begun in the Spirit, are you now being made perfect by the flesh?***

Foolish does not necessarily indicate a lack of intelligence but the lack of godly wisdom. Paul wonders if some kind of evil spell had prevented the Galatians from remembering the gospel of the **crucified** Christ, which had been clearly preached to them. He then contrasts obedience to the law with faith. Perhaps he had in mind Romans 20:17 when he said, *"So then faith comes hearing, and hearing the Word of God."* The Greek word for **"hear"** can also be translated **"listen"** or **"obey"** (see Romans 1:5; 16:26).

- Paul reminds the Galatians that their Christian life was **begun in the Spirit** by **grace** through faith alone (see v. 2; 2:16).

- He had seen that the Galatians were mistakenly trying to **be made perfect through the flesh** or achieve perfection [sanctification] through their own efforts [as perceived through their five senses] particularly at that time through circumcision.

If salvation is of the Lord and it is, then, it is of **grace** in its entirety, meaning:

- Believers are saved by **grace** through faith.

- Believers are justified by **grace** through faith.

- Believers are sanctified by **grace** through faith.

- Believers are glorified by **grace** through faith.

Christians are too conscious of sin [walking on egg shell syndrome] and too unconscious of **grace!** The revelation which formed the Protestant churches had as its objective the *Restoration* of all the truths of God's Word lost during the Medieval, Dark Ages of the Church. Historians named it the *Reformation*.

Restoration and reformation are probably distant cousins, but they are two very different words in meaning. Restoration refers to the *original state* [restored with original materials, while the reformation refers to *improving or fixing up* [with replacement materials not necessarily of the original materials].

From the very beginning with the reformers and state churches before them; the Church fathers wrote creeds, laws, and rules of order and conduct to guide the church, which through the years have evolved into an agenda void of the Churches' biblical purpose and mission, the Great Commandments [love "agape"] and the Great Commission ["to make disciples"]. They left their first love, Jesus Christ!

Evangelism [soul-winning] and edification [making disciples] are considered old fashioned, no longer relevant to the presumed needs of many churches today:

- In order to pursue their agenda the culture and many traditional churches across this nation have denied the Bible as the infallible Word of God; and have forfeited the biblical world-view, Christ-given mission and biblical purpose for existence.

- Like the Galatians they are turning their backs on the finished work of the **crucified** Christ, which has been **clearly portrayed** and **preached** to them.

- **It was Christ** who commanded that His disciples go into "all" the world and preach the gospel to every creature (Mark 16:15).

- **It was Christ** who commanded that His disciples "go" and "make disciples" of all nations, baptizing them in the name of the Father and of the Son and of the Holy Spirit, "teaching them to observe all things that I have commanded you . . ." (study Matthew 28:19).

- **It was Christ** who promised His presence with us (His disciples) even to the end of the age (v. 20).

- **It was Christ** who promised that we (His disciples) shall receive **power** [supernatural power] when the Holy Spirit has come upon you [us]; and you shall be witnesses of Me in Jerusalem [your family], and in all Judea and Samaria [your community and other areas of influence which incorporates all races and ethnicity] and to the "end of the earth" (see Acts 1:8). Brackets are mine.

I realize that some of the truths of God's Word; which I will be discussing in this book will ruffle some feathers individually and corporately; however, those points will be authenticated with the Scriptures. Pray with me and let's trust Christ for "**grace and truth.**" Are you and your Church on purpose and mission today?

I have added a study guide at the end of each chapter; to help reinforce and stabilize your daily walk with God while applying these truths of God's Word.

Jay R. Leach
Fayetteville, North Carolina

SECTION I

GRACE IN CRISIS

CHAPTER 1

LET'S GET IT RIGHT (GRACE)

*"For by **grace** you are saved through faith, and
that not of yourselves: it is the gift of God, not
of **works,** lest any man should boast"*
(Ephesians 2:8, 9).

Grace seems too good to be true! Why hasn't this been taught to us before? This is the typical response from Christians who have attended many of the traditional churches for years when confronted with the truths of God's Word concerning [grace], the finished work of Jesus Christ. It does seem too good to be true. But it is true! *Liberty, freedom, joy, passion, hope* and every spiritual and material blessing are produced by a true *revelation* of grace.

Unmerited Favor

"Salvation is of the Lord" (Jonah 2:9), therefore salvation is by **grace**. "And if by grace, then it is not by works" (Romans 11:6). Most of us are very familiar with the definition of grace as *"unmerited favor of God."* But through the truths of God's Word, *revealed* as we read the account of Jesus' suffering as foretold by the prophets and in the Psalms (and fulfilled in the Gospels) we realize that we can give only a limited definition of grace. In Titus 3:4, 5 we can define grace as "the kindness and love of God our Savior toward humankind . . . . Not by works of righteousness which we have done."

In the Scriptures, grace is contrasted or set against the Law of Moses. Under the Law of Moses, God **demanded** righteousness from *man;* but under grace, God in Christ **gives** righteousness to *man.* John 1:17 says, "The law was given by Moses, but *grace* and *truth* came by Jesus Christ." Yes, Jesus Christ is grace—and becomes ours by faith.

The Most Powerful Message

The most powerful and liberating message ever given to the human race is the Gospel of **grace**. It is the foundation upon which the Christian's redemption and life is established. This wonderful truth emphasizes what Christ did *for us* on the cross and what the Holy Spirit does *in us* in our daily lives. Keep these phrases in focus throughout your study of this book, (for us) and (in us).

The apostle Paul declares that we have become new creations in Christ, which has great implications for our lives. "Therefore, if anyone is in Christ, he [or she] is a new creation; old things have passed away . . . . all things have become new . . . . That we [in our regenerated spirits] might become the righteousness of God in Him" (Study 2 Corinthians 5:17-21). Christ has taken our sins and given us His righteousness (v. 21). Notice what the apostle Peter has to say about it. He writes, "**Grace** and **peace** be multiplied **to you** in the knowledge of God and of Jesus our Lord, as His **divine power** has given to us **all things** that pertain to **life** and **godliness**, through the knowledge of Him who called us by glory and virtue, by which have been given to us exceedingly great and precious promises, that **through these** you may be partakers of the divine nature, having escaped the corruption that is in the world through lust" (2 Peter 1:2-3). This describes our *new **legal** position* in Christ—how God sees and relates to us."

In Christ, all things have become new pertaining to *our spirit*. This includes:

- being fully accepted by God,
- receiving the authority to use the name of Jesus
- and the *indwelling* Holy Spirit;

Who is forming our new nature in the image of Christ—all of which enables us to resist the devil, sin, and sickness. We can now walk in victory releasing the works of God through supernatural intervention of prayer.

The Old Things passed away

This legal position includes:

- No longer being under the *penalty of sin.*
- No longer being dominated by the *power of sin.*

We have now reached a very crucial point; as the old saying goes, "where the rubber meets the road!" When we have been born again in our spirit, something has to take place in our soul and body to bring them into proper alignment with our regenerated spirit. Without proper alignment through renewal of our souls and bodies, we will remain carnal at best (see Romans 7:18).

We are familiar with the story told by many to illustrate this point. In the story a villager owned two dogs one was black and the other brown. Each Saturday afternoon, he would take the dogs to the village square to take bets and let them fight. He always won. One day an inquirer asked, "How is it that you always know which dog will win?" He answered, "The one I feed the most always wins." The dogs, one symbolizing the flesh and the other symbolizing the spirit—the one we *feed* the most will *always* win!

Should we continue in sin?

In Romans 6:1, Paul addresses this question of which dog to feed, beginning with a question. "What shall we say then? Shall we continue in sin that *grace* may abound? As if to say, "If God's grace is in proportion to a man or woman's sin, abounding most where sin abounds most—*shall we deliberately go on sinning that God's grace may abound toward us all the more?* "Is this the way we are supposed treat God's grace toward sinners?" Paul points out that this thinking is based on a *complete misunderstanding* of how God's grace *operates.* He elaborates:

- In order for a sinner to access God's grace there must be a **definite**, *personal* transaction *by faith* between the sinner and God.

- The nature of that transaction is so **profound** that it *produces a total transformation* within the personality of the sinner.

There are two opposing, but mutually complementary side effects to this transformation produced by God's **grace** in the sinners' personality:

- First there is a death—to sin and the old life!
- Second there is a new life—a life lived to God and to righteousness.

I can't emphasize enough the importance of your understanding these facts concerning the way in which grace through faith operates in the sinner. As a result of grace through faith we are faced with two alternative possibilities:

- If we **have** personally appropriated by faith God's grace on His terms—we are dead to sin.
- If we **are not** dead to sin, then, we have not appropriated by faith God's grace on His Word.

It is illogical and impossible to say that you have received God's grace, while at the same time practicing or living in sin. These two facts can **never** go together. Paul points out this truth in Romans 6:2: *"Certainly not! How shall we who died to sin live any longer in it?"* God's Word explicitly says "we have died to sin."

   This situation can be pictured through a true to life experience. I had just closed out the Sunday morning worship service, when I was summoned to the home of a congregant down the street from the church. She had just arrived home from our worship service. Her husband in a drunken state very abusive toward his family and definitely had no use for the Lord, tried to walk up the steps. He fell backwards, dead with a bottle of liquor in his coat pocket.

   While we waited for the County coroner and police—there he lays; the bottle had fallen out of his coat and lay beside him. He made absolutely no attempt to retrieve the bottle of liquor; neither was he cursing, and why not? He was dead—dead to cursing, dead to anger and dead to liquor.

- Sin no longer has any attraction for him.
- Sin no longer produces any reaction from him.
- Sin no longer has any power over him.

This is the picture of the **truth** of God's Word and the man, woman, girl or boy who has appropriated God's grace by faith. Through the operation of that **grace** [God's unmerited favor] that person has become dead to sin.

- Sin no longer has any attraction for him or her.
- Sin no longer produces any reaction from him or her.
- Sin no longer has any power over him or her.

Unlike this man—the believer is alive to God and His righteousness. Therefore, **grace** is the favor of God that gives us **access** to the **power of God** for everything we need for life and godliness. Did you get that saints? [Through **grace** we have **access** to the power of God!].

Who Himself bore our sins in His own body on the tree, that we, having <u>died to sin</u> might live to righteousness—by His stripes we are healed (1 Peter 2:24).

Crucified and Resurrected with Christ

The fact that the true Christian is through *God's grace*, dead to sin, can be found in numerous locations throughout the New Testament:

Knowing this, that our old man was crucified with Him, that the body of sin might be done away with; through death, that we should no longer be slaves of sin. For he who has died has been set free [justified] from sin (Romans 6:6-7).

7

Being *justified* by grace, because of Christ alone, through faith alone means that we are declared righteous because of what Christ has done for us—not because we have accepted what Christ has done. Did you get that? Read it again.

Paul is saying of each person who has accepted the atoning death of Christ, their old sinful nature, the old man, is crucified:

- The body of sin has been done away with.
- That person has been freed (justified) from sin.
- There is no longer any need to be the slave of sin.

Later in the same chapter; Paul repeats the teaching:

*Likewise you also, reckon yourselves to be dead indeed to sin, but alive to God in Christ Jesus our Lord. Therefore do not let sin reign in your mortal body, that you should obey it in its lusts . . . For sin **shall not** have dominion over you, for you are not under **law** but under **grace*** (Romans 6:11-12, 14; also see Romans 8:10).

Again, the meaning is plain:

- As true Christians we are to reckon ourselves as dead to sin through the **grace of God** in Christ Jesus.
- As a result, there is no reason why sin should continue to exercise any control or dominion over us.
- Later in another chapter, Paul reemphasizes the same truth again:

And if Christ is in you, the body is dead because of sin, but the Spirit is life because of righteousness (Romans 8:10).

Listen to the Word, *"if Christ is in you,"* this can only apply to the true Christian in whose heart Christ dwells by faith. Where Christ dwells, Satan certainly cannot! Two biblical truths are brought forth in this text:

- A death of the old carnal nature [the body] that is, the body of sin is dead—so bury it.
- A new life to righteousness through the operation of God's Spirit—the Spirit is life because of righteousness.

Dead bodies must be buried

Even though the old man is dead, the influence from his or her [body of sin] must be put away; otherwise the believer can be drawn back into old habits, behaviors and disobedience. We need deliverance from:

- The lusts of the flesh.
- The lusts of the eye.
- The pride of life.
- Thoughts of the old life.
- The works of the flesh.
- The sinful influences and habits of the old life.
- Psychological and physiological problems through Satan's constant accusations, past sins, inferior complexes, low esteem problems, abuse, insults, hurts, doubts and fears.

Only the Holy Spirit and the Word of God are capable of rooting these things out of born-again people. The major problem produced by this situation is that many of these people think or are led to believe that it is okay to continue in disobedience and sin because they are no longer under the law, but under grace. In the Garden of Eden, Adam knew the truth, yet sin came in. Ever since sin appeared absolute truth has been distorted; therefore man can no longer find absolute truth apart from God. Sin distorted all of the human faculties and now because of their sin natures, both men and women want to be the captain of their own ships, without God. Unfortunately, by the flesh [natural tendencies] of humans to distort truth, the fundamental biblical truths of **grace** have been lost. The tentacles of these natural tendencies have far-reaching implications.

The Bible never divorces faith in God's grace from obedience to His commands.

Let's consider a few passages of Scripture that **link** faith with obedience:

- He who believes in the Son has eternal life; and *he who does not* **believe the Son** *shall not see life,* but the wrath of God abides on him (John 3:36).
- Through Jesus we have received **grace** and apostleship to bring about *the obedience of faith* among all the Gentiles for His name's sake (Romans 1:5).
- For by *grace* you have been saved through faith; and that not of yourselves it is the gift of God . . . . (Ephesians 2:8b).

Obedience to the Lord's commands is the visible result of grace through faith. It has become the central *crisis* for the church today, as the cultures of many traditional churches across America have collapsed, due to the loss of true grace as they adhere to and promote the error of works—salvation or religious Christianity. This equates to dead works when not done in the power of the Holy Spirit.

Jude to the Rescue

Jude faced this great spiritual crisis in his day as he exhorted believers to contend *earnestly* for "**the faith**" or for the message of **grace** *originally* delivered to the saints (see Jude 3). For certain men have crept in unnoticed . . . . *ungodly men,* who turned the **grace** of our God into lewdness." Within *one generation* after Christ's resurrection, true grace had already been compromised and soon lost or ignored.

Satan at this point changed his strategy from that of being a roaring lion in the street [*persecution*], back to the serpent [*deception*], slithering into the church unnoticed *in* his people. Today these men and women creep in as angels of light [*false teachers*] in for the express purpose *to turn the message of grace into a message*

10

of lewdness or one that affirms various compromises and false teachings. These persuasive teachers twist what God's Word says about grace—into error thus, empowering many to boldly continue in sin, and sinful lifestyles without feeling any <u>urgency to repent!</u>

In reality, they have taken these verses out of context of the broader New Testament message, which calls for all believers *to live in wholehearted **love for Jesus*** as evidenced by seeking *to live in **obedience to Him*** (see John 14:15, 21). Today this method is enhanced by the lack of antithesis discourses; which demands both sides of the argument. If we preach or teach about heaven then we should teach about hell also. Out of such a discourse choice and hope are possible.

However, these false teachers preach and teach:

- Mostly on forgiveness without repentance.
- Receiving the blessings of the Lord on their circumstances without any conditions.
- Emphasizes only God's love.
- Ignores Jesus' call for commitment to the Lord.

The wonderful truth is, we are freely forgiven by Jesus and He blesses our circumstances. However, these truths are in conjunction with seeking to live in a *real and right relationship with Him,* and in agreement with His Lordship and in obedience to His Word. The sad truth is many believers aren't even cognizant of this crisis in the local churches concerning the *distorted **grace** message.*

Then there is a faction of the church that is in denial, with the thought; if anything is wrong—it will eventually straighten itself out, they think! Much conflict concerning grace can also be traced to misunderstanding the differences between these truths. Our Christian lives relate to our growing in righteousness which progresses as our minds, emotions, and wills are renewed and transformed through the Word of God and our Spirit-formed new nature (Romans 1:5).

The strength and stability of a society are related directly to the strength and stability of the authentic biblically based church.[1]

Russell Kirk, a brilliant political theorist and author, said of America and the West, *"Fundamentally, our society's affliction is the decay of religion."* If a culture is to survive and flourish, it must not be severed from the religious vision out of which it arose. He goes on to suggest that the necessity of reflective men and women, then, is to labor for *restoration of religious teachings as a credible body of doctrine.*[2]

In his book, *Cries of the heart,* Ravi Zacharias says, "Our commitment to God has sufficient objective truth so that the truth claims can be verified. He further states, there are historical, geographical, and philosophical assertions that can be measured and confirmed by the historian, the archeologist, and the philosopher, respectively.[3] The Scriptures remind us that God has graciously invited us to come to Him on a personal level.

"Come to me, all of you who are tired and have heavy loads, and I will give you rest. Accept my teachings and learn from me, because I am gentle and humble in spirit, and you will find rest for your lives" (Matthew 11:28) NCV.

There are no exceptions to God's invitation. His electing, redeeming, calling **grace** does not exclude anyone. However, God's grace includes people who would otherwise exclude themselves. The sovereign grace of God insures that the invitation will be successful so that people will respond. *For "No one can come to me unless the Father who sent Me draws him [or her]"* (John 6:44).

Study Questions (Chapter 1)

1. "Salvation is of the Lord" (Jonah 2:9), therefore salvation is by _____." (PG. 10)

2. Under the Law of Moses, God demanded _____ from man, but under _____ God in Christ gives _____ to man. (PG. 10)

3. In order for a sinner to have a definite transaction with God; what must take place? (PG. 11)

4. We are _____ ____ _____ if we have personally appropriated by faith God's grace on His terms. (PG. 12)

5. "If Christ is in you" two biblical truths are brought forth in Romans 8:10. (PG.13)
    •
    •

6. Explain in detail below Jude's exhortation to the saints concerning the "ungodly men." (PG. 15)

7. How do believers compare today with these first century believers? (PG. 16) Explain:

CHAPTER 2

TO BE OR NOT TO BE

A word that I love in reference to preaching and teaching is "antithesis" which is defined as the opposition, contrast of ideas or the direct opposite.[4] We hear a lot of one destination preaching and teaching today. One preaches everyone is going to heaven, and others are even saying that after death we all receive wings and become angels. In the movies, Hollywood makes evil angels heroes and good; while at the same time portraying good angels as evil. The Bible is under such violent attack in today's society; it would seem that many would want to check it out and compare, just out of curiosity. It is so sad that many in the local churches believe and spout this malarkey. The truth of God's Word is by no means inclusive, as secular society would love it to be—you must be born again!

Saint or Sinner

The Scripture says, *"There is therefore now no condemnation to those who are in Christ Jesus, who do not walk according to the flesh, but according to the Spirit. The law of the Spirit of life in Christ has made me free from the law of sin and death"* (Romans 8:1, 2).

"Therefore" refers back to 7:25, a condition which has almost become the norm in many local churches. People want to claim v.1 and lay aside what Paul says in contrast in the preceding vivid description of sinfulness.

In Romans 8:1, Paul assures the saints that they are not under condemnation in Christ, nor are they under the sentence of the law—however, their newly brought to life spirits are **empowered** by the indwelling Holy Spirit, to **live** for Christ.

That is why the Scripture reiterates and makes it so vividly clear, *"But you are not in the flesh but in the Spirit, if indeed the Spirit of God dwells in you. Now if anyone does not have the Spirit of Christ, he [or she] is not His"* (Romans 8:9). Emphasis added.

You can't have both

Many Christians and local churches are ignoring or have not taken this passage (Romans 8:7-11) very seriously. A Christian can live according to the flesh with the results of death (see James 1:13-15), or by the regenerated spirit and experience life. In verses 7-11, Paul elaborates on these two possibilities—showing the possibility and the benefit of living according to the Spirit.

Another growing condition in the local churches is carnal-mindedness. In verse 7, Paul informs that being carnally-minded results in death (v. 6). Additionally, the carnal mind is the **enemy** of God. The mind of the **flesh [controlled by the five senses]** is hostile to God and can never submit itself to the law of God.

There was a day when the so-called "revolving door" in churches served sinners and hypocrites; however, today many true saints are leaving the churches in grief; as the churches forfeit their Christ-given mission to "make disciples" and "extend the kingdom of God" on earth. Many of these churches are yielding to or being absorbed into the secular culture. Others find themselves wresting with issues the church is facing that demands a stand for biblical truth. I read an article concerning a same sex married couple who expressed their desire to join a church and the pastor refused them based on the church's biblical worldview. One of the other area pastors, when asked about the incident by a national press reporter remarked, "That pastor has a very **narrow** and **bigoted** point of view." "You need to consider all points of view!" I'm not sure the pastor who made those compromising remarks considered *the* fact that only one point of view counts—God's! As expressed with vivid clearness in His inerrant Word [The Holy Bible]. Some other churches have simply become "Come one come all entertainment centers."

Many churches create religious programs, annual events and secular activities to fill the void created by the absence of the Holy Spirit and a biblical worldview; yet they remain within their own comfort zones "be and act like us" communities or you are the enemy.

Again I say, "Such churches have actually given up their reason for existence, since their present agenda and behavior require a forfeiture of their biblical purpose and mission. I call this religious Christianity. Let me sum up my point here with an illustration:

A pastor was preparing his Sunday sermon as his young son watched him. After a while the little boy asked, "Daddy I thought you said God gives you the sermon." He does give me the sermon son." Well dad if God gives you the sermon, "why are you doing all of that erasing?"

A doctor may correct his or her diagnosis, philosophers may correct thoughts of their own invention, but no servant of the Word [preacher] has the authority to correct the inerrant word of God— the Bible. Conformity with the world is enmity with God!

We will explore this at length in chapter 9, as we cover Secular humanism's philosophy. Young people today expect a better reality-answer then that! The Bible tells it like it is; and we are obligated to let it speak the truth in love, at times [tough love] through us!

The church that stops rescuing the lost—needs to be rescued!

Paul counseled the Galatians concerning similar conditions:

*O foolish Galatians! Who has bewitched you that you should **not obey the truth,** before whose eyes Jesus Christ was clearly portrayed among you as crucified? This only I want to learn from you: Did you receive the Spirit by the works of the law, or by the hearing of faith? **Are you so foolish? Having begun in the Spirit, are you now being made perfect in the flesh?***

One of the main points of Paul's letter to the Galatians and to the church today is:

Hear what the Spirit is saying to the churches! Justification which means declared [righteous or pardoned] is **only** by **grace** through faith in the "finished work of Jesus Christ." Any other way allows

works, whether it is by keeping the Law of Moses or by performing good deeds—to play a role in justification.

If righteousness is attainable through keeping the Law of Moses or good deeds and works, then God's **gracious** act of sending Jesus to die on the cross to pay for our sins was **unnecessary** and useless (see Romans 3:4-26).

Grace versus Law

The Galatian believers were under pressure from Jewish **legalists** and were considering rejecting the **Gospel of Grace** and reverting back to dependence on the **Mosaic Law** for salvation. Please study the following verses concerning Law and Grace:

1. Under the Law there was a dividing veil (Exodus 26:33).
    Grace brought a rent veil (Hebrews 10:19-22).

2. Law blots out the sinner (Ex0dus 32:33).
    Grace blots out the sinner's sin (Colossians 2:14).

3. The Law curses the offender (Galatians 3:10).
    Grace covers the offender (Romans 4:7).

4. The Law cries out, "Do—and live!" (Deuteronomy 8:1).
    Grace cries out, "It is done! It is finished! Receive Jesus and live!" (John 19:30; John 1:12).

5. The Law cries out, "Every mouth opened stopped" (Romans 3:19).
    Grace invites, "Every mouth opened . . . that if you confess with your mouth the Lord Jesus and believe in your heart that God has raised Him from the dead, you will be saved" (Romans 10:9). "Whoever calls on the name of the Lord shall be saved" (Romans 10:13).

6. The Law showed favor to the good (Proverbs 12:2).
    The Grace of God shows mercy and favor to the bad, the ungodly (Ephesians 2:1-6).

7. The Law was given upon stone . . . outward (II Corinthians 3:3).
    Grace is graven on the heart . . . inward . . . Christ in you
    (Colossians 1:27; 3:3; II Corinthians 3:3).

8. The Law says, "He added no more" (Deuteronomy 5:22).
    Grace of God assures us, "He has spoken to us by His Son"
    (Hebrews 1:2).

9. Law is inexorable in its demand (Joshua 7:25).
    The Grace of God is inspirational in its blessing (II
    Corinthians 5:17).

10. The Law brings judgment (Romans 5:18).
    Grace brings justification (Roman 3:24).

11. Law cries out, "Keep the Commandments—all of them, in
    every minute detail" (James 2:10).
    Grace assures us we are kept by the power of God (I
    Peter 1:5).

12. The Law demands love (Deuteronomy 6:5).
    The Grace of God exhibits love (John 3:16).

13. The Law moves the sinner to sin (Romans 7:8).
    The Grace of God removes sin from the sinner (Matthew 1:21).

14. According to the Law, nearness to God is impossible
    (Exodus 20:21).
    In Grace, nearness to God is guaranteed (Ephesians 2:13).

15. The Law demands obedience—or no blessing (Deuteronomy
    28:1-2).
    Grace brings obedience because of the blessing (I John 4:19).

16. The Law cries out, "Stone the prodigal" (Deuteronomy
    21:20-21).
    Grace cries out, "Put the best robe on the prodigal . . . kill
    the fatted calf! Let us feast and be merry!" (Luke 15:20-22).

17. Law brings death (Deuteronomy 21:20-23).
Grace gives to us the quietness and assurance of peace (Romans 5:1).

18. The Law retaliates (Exodus 21:24).
The Grace of God redeems (Galatians 3:13).

19. The Law *demands* sanctification (Leviticus 11:44).
Grace *bestows* sanctification (I Corinthians 1:30).

20. Because of the Law, three thousand were slain (Exodus 32:28).
Because of the Grace of God, three thousand were saved (Acts 2:41).

21. The Law is unsatisfying to the conscience (Hebrews 10:1-2).
The Grace of God is unfailing in its forgiveness and remedy for sin (Hebrews 9:12-14; 10:10-14).

22. The Law is the voice of consternation (Hebrews 12:18-21).
The Grace of God is the voice of covenant, blessing, peace and assurance (Hebrews 12:22-24).

23. When the Law was given, Moses' face shown, and the people feared (Exodus 34:30).
Grace brought by Jesus Christ attracted the people to the face of Jesus (Mark 9:15).

24. The Law was a yoke of burdensome weight (Galatians 5:1).
Grace is to be in the yoke with Jesus, which makes the yoke easy and the burden light (Matthew 11:29-30).

25. The Law produced zeal (Roman 10:1-2, but no salvation (Philippians 3:6; Romans 10:1-8).
Grace imparts zeal, and brings joy unspeakable and full of glory because we are saved (Titus 2:14; I Peter 1:8).[5]

I am so grateful that **"Christ is the end of the Law for righteousness to everyone that believes."**

Notice these precious blessings—all are the results of God's grace:

- We are "accepted in the beloved" (Ephesians 1:6).
- We are "blessed with all spiritual blessings" (Ephesians 1:3).
- We are called the sons of God (1 John 3:1).
- We are delivered from the wrath to come (I Thessalonians 1:10).
- We are the elect of God (I Thessalonians 1:4).
- We are forgiven by God (Ephesians 1:7) for Christ's sake (Ephesians 4:32).
- We are saved by the grace of God (Ephesians 2:5).
- We are a holy priesthood (I Peter 2:5).
- We are hidden in Christ (Colossians 3:3).
- We are justified in His sight without works (Romans 3:28).
- We are kept for Jesus Christ (Jude 1).
- Life eternal is given to us by Jesus (John 10:28).
- We are near to God by the blood of His Son (Ephesians 2:13).
- We are ordained to eternal life (Acts 13:48).
- We have peace with God (Romans 5:1).
- We are quickened together with Christ (Ephesians 2:5).
- We are redeemed to God by Christ's blood (Revelation 5:9).

To be or not to be

Paul's example in telling the Galatians the **truth,** signals a wake-up call for all true churches and believers today. Some so-called enlightened philosophical Christian writers have attempted to bring biblical truth in line with current cultural norms and ideas. This is a blatant attack on the Bible. Collapsing under this satanic attack says much about our authenticity as true lovers of God and our fellow human beings. American Christianity appears to prefer the political model of non-partisanship; which is nothing but old-fashioned compromise. Knowing that to do so is in direct violation of the Great Commandment; which in turn annuls the Great Commission.

"The mouth of a righteous man [or woman] is a well of life" (Proverbs 10:11a)

So much of the American Church for the most part continues the long-standing policy of following the Traditional and Institutional Churches' doctrines, customs and traditions over biblical doctrine and revelation of the present truth of God's Word **[Which I repeat is restoration of biblical truths lost during the Dark Ages].** Many churches are adopting the ideas of secular humanism which holds that there are no absolutes and therefore, all truth is relative. We are in the world but not of it. As children of God, we believe in objective truth—Jesus is objective truth in fact, He is "The Truth!" Anything else offered has to be subjective. The battle for the "truth" of God's Word personally and corporately rages as local churches grapple with secular positions and ideas which attempt to stretch the biblical worldview beyond measure. One of the Holy Spirit's ministries for His Church is to lead and guide us into all truth. Jesus said, *"When He, the Spirit of truth, has come, He will **guide you into all truth;** for He will not speak on His own authority, but whatever He hears He will speak; and will **tell you** things to come"* (John 16:13).

Objective versus Subjective Truth

One parishioner remarked, "Pastor I feel that I am both objective and subjective when interpreting God's Word." Trying to be on both sides is error. When taking no one position is also a position—double-mindedness! What do those words really mean anyway?

1. Objective—means outside and independent of the mind. So looking at the truth of God's Word objectively is seeing the body of real events or facts as they really are without distortion by personal feelings or prejudices.[6]
2. Subjective—means relating to or arising within one's own self or mind in contrast to what is outside.[7] Subjective truth then is my personal interpretation in spite of the real events or facts.

The apostle Paul was taken aback by the Galatians. In spite of his preaching of the gospel of "grace"; his personal testimony and life-living before them, they had a zeal for the Law of Moses and the traditions of their fathers which had blinded them from **grace** and **truth.** Many churches today are still listening to the teaching and are following their founders' century old vision, accessed only through the rearview mirror; thoroughly oblivious of what the Spirit is saying to the churches today. These churches are following second-hand religious Christianity, subjective beliefs and church doctrines. I repeat; Paul was disappointed with the Galatians. He asked the question, "What you have begun in the Spirit, are you going to finish it in the flesh?"

In this church setting, one is saved by **grace** through **faith**—but now for the rest of your life, you must try your best to be on good behavior to please God and be blessed. So off you go on the road to sanctification actually attempting the impossible over and over again to try please God through your performance:

- Dress like us,
- Act like us God will be pleased.
- You are expected to tithe your total entitlement, not just the net.
- The Bible says; fail not to assemble yourselves together, so we'll be looking for you every Sunday.
- Work to please God!
- I have some advice for you! The Bible is full of rules, so read it daily for instruction on how to act.

A check of church history reveals that the major leaders of the Reformation, both Luther and Calvin took this approach, one is saved by **grace through faith,** but then for the rest of our earthly lives we are to try to modify our behavior and live right in our natural strength. Now five hundred years later, for the most part the American Church continues to take that approach.

Upon visiting most Protestant Churches, you will probably hear and see in action a mixture of *law* and *grace.* This "saved by grace, but sanctified by human effort" approach produces churches with many of its Christians *caught up* in sins of the flesh *[works of the flesh],* as recorded in (Galatians 5:19-21):

- Adultery
- Fornication
- Uncleanness
- Lewdness
- Idolatry
- Sorcery
- Hatred
- Contentions
- Jealousies
- Outbursts of wrath
- Selfish ambitions
- Dissensions
- Heresies
- Envy
- Murders
- Drunkenness
- Revelries

Paul ends this list of sins with, [*"and the like,"*] meaning this list is not complete. He concludes with, *". . . . those that **practice** such things **will not** inherit the kingdom of heaven"* (v. 21). As I began this section, I said Christians commit through immaturity, spiritual ignorance, satanic deception, and many times a part of the flesh that we know is there, but we don't seek deliverance from it and one day Satan uses it to ruin our testimony. Those who have begun in the Spirit, but strive to walk in their own strength make themselves easy prey for the works of the flesh.

The Christian life is supernatural, therefore such a life is positive proof that those persons caught up in the works of the flesh are not living in the power of the Holy Spirit (see vv. 16, 18, 22, 23), but being influenced and energized by Satan and his hosts (see Matthew 16:13; Acts 5:3). Close the door! The desires of the flesh are at odds with the **Holy Spirit's** desire that we be free from sin. Paul's bottom line or admonition is for believers to avoid and overcome these sinful character killers and: "Walk in the Spirit, and you **shall not** fulfill the lusts of the flesh" (see v. 16).

Aiding and Abetting

The Scripture says, "Those who **practice** the works of the flesh **shall not inherit the kingdom of God.**" The word **PRACTICE** is the key in Paul's warning. The local churches' membership is not like "one size fits all" caps, socks, etc. Those persons in the membership who practice—this verb describes a *continual or habitual action* (see 1 John 3:9). In the prior section I stated that true Christians may find themselves *caught up* in these same sins. I use the phrase caught up, because it characterizes how the true believer arrives there by opening a door and Satan enters. But the true believer **cannot** remain there [*for it is no longer his or her nature*]. However, the love for God, His glory, other people, the Holy Spirit's conviction [convincing], remorse and repentance along with the accompanying downward spiral sets in motion actions and a desire to be set free from this sin.

These people need help! They need to be lovingly shown the way out. What they don't need is condemnation; which is the norm in much of the traditional and institutional church in America. Many times these folks are only faithful in coming to the Sunday morning service [one in the crowd]. They don't necessarily dress and act according to the church's tradition. However, after the service is over Satan's old demonic oppression and accusation return therefore blocking any thought or attempt of change in the person. For many their condition and circumstances are like fish in water— that's all there is! With that in view, "how will this affect the next generation's churches?"

The Great Emergence
It is imperative that the churches *be reminded* that Jesus came to set the captives free (see Luke 4:18). He also said that we would carry on *His* Ministry (see John 14:12). We tend to forget that the Church is intended to be a hospital-like conduit, serving the kingdom of God by *healing* people **spiritually, emotionally, and physically—like Jesus did.** Unless the churches deliberately bring the power of Jesus

through the Holy Spirit into the church's purpose and mission they have only human power trying to solve superhuman problems. This may give some help—but not healing. Therefore these people come to church week after week and depart continuing to suffer under Satan's fiery darts of: *oppression, depression, fear, unbelief, evil thoughts, emotional and mental torment, satanic accusations and deception.*

The exodus of young people from the local churches where they were raised; became disappointed as they constantly heard the Word preached and taught all their lives, but saw very little [reality] of fleshing out that word in the church's daily experiences. I am often asked to explain young people to the older generations—I really enjoy the task. I assure them, all is not lost and by no means has Christ forfeited His church to the devil. Never! Therefore, the Holy Spirit has a bull-pin full of young leaders warming up in training and receiving vision for His new wineskin in the next generation.

In fact many of them are already at work in this generation. They'll do fine for whatever is required for them to do the task, will be accomplished through the Holy Spirit and the word of God. God will pour out His anointing into those whom He has truly chosen and called, just as He has done for prior generations. As *anointed* old wineskins we are to be their launching pads for the new wine. For a successful launch there is checklist to be completed at the pad, to name a few:

- He or she must be anointed and appointed by the Holy Spirit.
- He or she must be trained and set on the right course (sound doctrine).
- He or she must be aware that none of the above can *be initiated* unless he or she knows Christ as *their* Savior and Lord—love Him and others.
- He or she must be walking in the Spirit through grace by faith in the finished work of Christ.
- He or she must be obedient to the Lord's commands.

While many churches do not have meaningful formal healing, biblical education and training ministries, much can be done in plain old loving and caring "one another" ministry through the study of the Bible focused holistically on the spiritual and physical needs of the person. God's Word heals! Jesus said, "If you ask anything in My name, I will do it" (John 14:14). The Church must acknowledge that shortcoming and begin teaching God's people a viable biblical worldview, the truths and promises of God's Word.

For the next generation, the lines between right and wrong, between truth and error, between Christian influence and cultural accommodation are increasingly **blurred**. While there are certainly challenges for every generation—*we have an open window of opportunity as church leaders to do something about this unique problem, otherwise the spiritual formation of tomorrow's church will be seriously threatened.*

Additionally, a present truth is a [*truth of God's Word ignored or hidden since being revealed in the Reformation*]—in this case that ignored truth is "the priesthood of all believers." People are the churches' most important resource and I might add many are untapped resources. This is probably the only war in existence where the soldiers are not trained to fight. It was always God's desire to be among His people. Jesus fleshed out what the Father had in mind even leaving His example for us in the Gospels.

The Holy Spirit is here to empower the leadership with a kingdom mind; for the task to be properly completed we must return to our Commander for His guidance through His Spirit and His Word. Then we must provide formal training for Holy Spirit-filled believers who can lead and participate in deeper life helping ministries. As priests all Christians are invited to come boldly to the **throne of Grace** where they have **access** to God's presence and power for everything we need; and it is imperative that these truths be communicated to the entire Church, with special embracing of the young people:

I have provided a list of possible suggestions for ministries below which may be used for examples; but is by no means exhaustive:

- Challenge the entire church to develop love for God and others, for biblical teaching with application and a viable biblical worldview.
- Biblical Counseling Ministry—There are many self-described counselors in the local churches, however proper training is available. Seek!

- Small group Ministry—(every believer should participate in a group for learning, nurture and sanctification). I believe this is the alternative for the faithful few who try to carry on the Wednesday night tradition of prayer meeting and Bible study.
- Accountability Ministry—no lone rangers need apply. We all need to be accountable to someone for periodic spiritual checkups.
- Mentorship and Family Life Ministry—(special focus should be on those 18-29 years olds). I believe this group deserves special attention because pluralism is causing a greater number of casualties today in this group then in past generations. Many even after significant exposure to biblical Christianity as children, teenagers, and young adults are missing from the pews and active commitment to Christ. Statistics reveal that of those churches effectively reaching these young people, the number reached is only a drop in the bucket, considering the number of young people who reside in their local community. Generations of young people in the past have left the church, but after marriage, entering a career or at least at some point returned. This generation is not returning and if they do return it may be to another faith![8]
- One out of every four young adults (27 percent) stated that they "grew up a Christian, but they perceive the church has kept them fearful and detached from the world." They look for excitement outside traditional boundaries. This may be pornography or sexual experimentation, drugs, internet, and extreme thrill seeking and some have tried other faiths or spiritual practices.[9]
- Spiritual gifts in Ministry—believers should be allowed to employ spiritual gifts in the local church. Spiritual gifts are not the individual's gift, but are resident in the Holy Spirit and given by Him to the Church for the good of all.
- Even in the smallest churches, associations, or unions there are gifted-teachers who can enlighten the saints on human development through small group, conferences or power point and other means. This will familiarize each generation

with the others and answer the why questions of each generation.

- Core teachings on the Doctrine of Christ found in (see Hebrews 6:1-6).
- Insure that every member knows the Church's purpose and mission [statement] to extend the kingdom of God on the earth.
- Special emphasis on each believer building a viable biblical worldview.
- Spiritually gifted persons prayerfully assigned to lead these ministries of Edification [spiritual growth to mature disciples] and **then** Evangelism [winning the lost].
- Insure that pastoral ministry is a shared task.
- Mark a clear distinction between Church work [in reach] and the work of the Church [outreach]. A decent budget should be established to meet ministry needs.

Many times wayward Christians come to Church seeking help, hoping and expecting healing or at least help through the "one another" areas of ministry, but nothing happens because the church; though we constantly preach and teach present truths; many are not applying them in everyday life nor the church. To keep it simple, many churches treat these struggling Christians just as they treat visitors, "glad to have you this morning, come again."

Soon they will drop out and begin to float. Many of these are families with children and I'm sure they wonder if it is worth all the bother, since they are not a priority?

A true saying concerning any sin: Sin will carry you further than you want to go. Keep you longer than you want to stay and cost you more than you want to pay!

I titled this section aiding and abetting because Christ's answer to not only this problem, but to all individual and Church problems is—**grace!** Romans 6:14 says, *"Sin shall not be master over you, for you are **not** under **law** but under **grace.**"*

In his book "Pure Grace," Clark Whitten comments, *"It is not by law keeping or disciplining our **flesh** that we overcome sin, experience an abundant life, or achieve any spiritual victory. It all begins with receiving **the abundance of grace!*** He continues, *"Most of us have been taught to be good givers, but few have been taught to be good receivers. Our **willingness and sense of liberty** to receive all Jesus died to give is the key here.*[10]

As I preach and teach grace, I have an uncomfortable feeling in my spirit; and I pray that I am not aiding and abetting the enemies of grace, who use it as a catch-all license to sin. I am careful in clarifying the Spirit-led teaching, because most people and churches are use to a form of **grace/law** rather than **grace alone through faith**. For so many people grace is "present truth" not new [as if never known] but the revelatory truth of God's Word **restored in these last days to the body of Christ.** Christ came into the world and died; thereby **satisfying** the Father's demands for sin! God is not angry with you, He is pleased and satisfied as a result of the finished work of His Son—and not anything we've done! That's grace! The Bible says,

But God demonstrates His own love toward us, in that while we were still sinners [His enemies], Christ died for us.

I am right with God. Jesus made it right for me and then presented it to me as a gift, **and I received it with love.** Notice the gift!

*That if you confess with your mouth the Lord Jesus and believe in your heart that God has raised Him from the dead, you will be saved. For with the heart one believes **unto righteousness,** and with the mouth confession is made unto salvation* (Romans 10:9-10).

Look at grace! I am as **righteous** at this very moment as I will be in heaven. I believe in my heart that God raised Jesus from the dead and confess with my mouth **Jesus is Lord,** resulting in **righteousness.**

*"He made Him who knew no sin to be sin on our behalf, so that we might become the righteousness of God **in Him"** (2 Corinthians 5:21).*

Righteousness is a state of being. I stand before God righteous or right with Him—based on who I am; and not what I have done or will do. It is by my Christ-earned **position [in Christ]**—not by any **performance** that I have done.

People in right standing with God do righteous deeds, but righteous deeds do not make a person righteous! There is only **one path** to righteousness and it is by **[grace]** through faith in Christ's finished work. Like the people in the church at Galatia, many Christians are going about today trying to establish their own righteousness based on keeping the law, again, this is religious Christianity—not the true Christianity. That is not the way it is with **grace!** I can reign with Christ by receiving this great gift of righteousness and knowing I have been **made righteous** because I believe Christ's finished work—not because I act right!

Remember, a person can do an unrighteous deed—but that unrighteous deed does not make him or her unrighteous. Why not? It's because righteousness is not based on any kind of deeds, but upon faith. So it is also with an unrighteous person, he or she can do a righteous deed, but the righteous deed will not make that person righteous. Righteousness is **who** I am **in Christ**—not **what** I do!

Access to the Power

As with so many truths of God's Word, people miss one of their greatest blessings, living the abundant life now, by either ignoring **grace** or making it complicated. The Spirit speaking through the apostle Peter, who writes,

*"Grace and peace be multiplied unto you in the **knowledge of God,** and of Jesus our Lord, as His divine power has given to us all things that pertain to life and godliness, through the knowledge of Him who called us by glory and virtue"* (2 Peter 1:2-3).

Grace then is the favor of God that gives us **access** to the **power of God** for everything we need for a life and godliness. Think about it! Grace is the undeserved, unearned favor of God that:

- Gives us access to the power of God for everything we need for life and godliness.
- Gives us the **legal right** to access the power of God for everything we need.
- None of us deserves access to God and His power (Romans 3:10, 23).
- Because of sin, we all deserve the everlasting lake of fire. Yet God has given us access to all He is and all He has. That's grace, folks!

God has shown us mercy by not making us pay the just penalty for our sin. In Christ, the mercy keeps us from the judgment we truly deserve. We are saved by grace [favor of God] without which we could never have **access** to the **mercy of God.** God favored us *while we were yet sinners.*

God first released His grace before He was able to extend His mercy to us. Romans 5:8 tells us, "But God demonstrates His own love toward us, in that while we were yet sinners, Christ died for us."

Notice these *truly important* facts concerning the **grace of God:**

- We didn't deserve the favor of God.
- We deserved hell.
- But God so loved us, and placed such value on us—even while we were **yet** His enemies.
- He sent Jesus, His only Son, to die for us—so that we might have *access* to Him.
- With this *access,* we can now receive mercy for *all* of our sins.

It is that access that we receive undeserved and unearned— that has allowed us to be forgiven, cleansed, and made a new creation (see II Corinthians 5:17). **It is also by that access we can receive His righteousness and receive mercy for all our sins** (see II Corinthians 5:21).

Grace is receiving what we do not deserve [favor]—while mercy is not receiving what we do justly deserve [death]!

Back to Eden

Satan's goal in the Garden of Eden was to introduce **sin** to the world [to all humanity] through Adam and Eve; which resulted in their no longer having *access* to the eternal power of God. Thus, *cutting off everything we would need for life and godliness.* He knew from **his own experience** that if Adam and Eve sinned, their access to the [tree of life] total provision and *continual supply* would cease.

The grace of God through the finished work of Jesus **gives back,** to those who are in Christ—the access to God's power for *everything we need.* Notice the Scriptural results we receive **through grace,** Christ's finished work:

- Justification
- Sanctification
- Glorification

All things considered

God has given you and me access to His very presence and power. Through His undeserved **favor,** God chose to give us everything we need for life and it comes **only** by grace—that means everything we need for life has *already* been given to us:

- Shelter
- Clothing
- Physical food
- Spiritual food
- Healing
- Relationships
- Finances

Strength to Stand

Through grace God has given each believer protection and strength to stand in full obedience against the devil and his demonic attacks [darts]. He has provided Spiritual armor for total [whole person] protection; which enables us to fully engage the enemy. It is by spiritual weapons that the Church is able to war a good warfare and be a part of that victorious Body against which the gates of hell shall not prevail (see Matthew 16:18-19).

- Jesus Christ is far above all principalities, powers and might and dominion. As believers we are complete in Him and seated with Him in heavenly places (see Ephesians 1:20-21).
- The New Testament reveals an invisible realm of evil powers, the kingdom of this world that deceives and manipulates human behavior; advancing Satan's strategy to wreck God's plans for humanity. This realm is involved in the circumstances each of us face daily.
- It is worthy to note that we have only one enemy—Satan! Our fellowman is our enemy only to the extent that he or she allows Satan to use them.

The Scripture says, *"We do not wrestle against flesh and blood, but against powers, against rulers of the darkness* [biblical and Spiritual ignorance] *of the age, against spiritual hosts of wickedness in heavenly places"* (Ephesians 6:12). Paul further admonishes us to, *"Put on the whole armor of God that you may be able to withstand in the evil day, and having done all, to stand"* (Ephesians 6:13).

- Jesus came to destroy the works of Satan therefore, by the grace of God, we are not to be passive, but on the offense against the enemy forces.
- Recognize that your demonic enemies are behind much of what comes against you.

In Ephesians 6:14-17, Paul listed six pieces of spiritual armor essential for each believer to be properly ready for battle:

- Loins girt about with **truth** (v. 14).
- Breastplate of **righteousness** (v. 14).
- Feet shod with the preparation of the **gospel of peace** (v. 15).
- The shield of **faith** (v. 16).
- The helmet of **salvation** (v. 17).
- The sword of the Spirit, the **Word of God.**

Prayer and Supplication

Paul's final counsel: We are to be *"praying with all prayer and supplication in the Spirit"* (v. 18).

- While prayer is not a part of the armor, it is the means through grace by which we engage the enemy.
- Prayer is the battle itself.
- God's Word, the chief offensive weapon is deployed during the struggle.
- Study Christ, our example in Matthew 4:1-11.

In Ephesians 1:17-18, Paul prayed that the people of God would receive "the Spirit of wisdom and revelation" with the duel objectives of:

1. Knowing Christ.
2. Understanding God's power and purpose in their lives.

Revelation here refers to an unveiling of our hearts that we may receive:

- Clear Perception
- Applicable wisdom
- An understanding of the Word of God
- Clear understanding of God's will for you
- Understand how God how God intended His Word to work in building our lives.

Key to God's Will

In Matthew 7:24-27, Jesus emphasized the importance of knowing and doing God's will:

"Therefore whoever hears these sayings of mine, and does them, I will liken him to a wise man who built his house on the rock: and the rain descended, the floods came, and the winds blew and beat on that house; and it did not fall, for it was founded on the rock.

But everyone who hears these sayings of Mine, and does not do them, will be like a foolish man who built his house on the sand: and the rain descended, the floods came, and the winds blew and beat on that house; and it fell. And great was its fall."

STUDY GUIDE: CHAPTER 2

1. Justification means declared _____. This can only happen by _____ through faith in the "_____ _____ of _____."(PG. 19)

2. The law of the _____ _____ in Christ has made me _____ from the _____ of sin and _____. (PG. 18)

3. A Christian can live according to the _____ __ with the results of _____. (PG. 18)

4. The mind of the _____ is hostile to God, and can never _____ itself to the law of God. (PG. 18)

5. Paul warned the Galatians, who had begun in the Spirit, but trying to _____ in the _____. (PG. 19)

6. _____ truth means outside and independent of the mind. (PG. 23)

7. _____ truth relates to its arising within one's self or mind in contrast to what is outside. (PG. 23)

8. Grace is the _____ _____ of God. (PG. 29)

9. Everything we need for life comes only by _____. (PG. 29)

10. List the six pieces of armor essential for spiritual warfare. (PG. 32)
    1.
    2.
    3.
    4.
    5.
    6.

CHAPTER 3

GRACE THAT SAVES

*"If by the transgression of the one, death reigned through the one, much more those who **receive the abundance of grace** and of the **gift of righteousness** through the One, Jesus Christ"*
(Romans 5:17).

When you wake up thinking about spiritual things and how you are doing in your walk with God, is your inventory of yourself based on your performance of works? If so I encourage you to lift your eyes up to Jesus Christ and His "finished work." We often hear individuals and even some churches continuously say, "I am [or we are] "working" to please Him! If that is your philosophy of the Christians' or Churches' life, then you and the church have ventured on to a life of "unfinished work" in the "flesh" that is unending.

Many Christians strive to act and look like the world, supposedly to win them to Christ. God through the Holy Spirit and the truths of His Word is transforming us into the likeness of His Son. Therefore, Christlikeness in our character and conduct draws people by the grace of God to Christ in us.

The Apostle Paul penned a statement that contrasts the results of Adam's sin with the results of the *righteous life, sacrificial death,* and *victorious resurrection* of Jesus Christ. He is saying in this statement, we **will** reign in life. Notice:

*Therefore, just as through one man [Adam] sin entered the world, and death through sin, and so death spread to all men, because all sinned—for until the Law sin was in the world; but sin is **not** imputed when there is **no** law. Nevertheless death reigned from Adam until Moses, even over those who had not sinned in the likeness of Adam's offense, who is a type of Him who was to come. But the **free gift** is not like the transgression. For if by the transgression of the one the many died, much more did the **grace of God** and the **gift by the grace** of the one Man, Jesus Christ, abound to the many. The **gift** is not like that which came through the* *one who sinned; for on the one hand the judgment arose from one transgression resulting in **condemnation,** but on the other hand the free gift arose from many transgressions resulting in **justification.** For if by the transgression of the one, death reigned through the one, much more those who **receive the abundance of grace** and of **the gift righteousness—will reign in life** through the **One, Jesus Christ"** (Romans 5:12-17). [Emphasis added].*

This passage says, "Will reign in life," and not "should reign in life." The Word of God, in many other places confirms this truth. *"We can do all things through Christ who strengthens us"* (see Philippians 4:13). *"We are more than conquerors—through Christ who loves us* (see Romans 8:37). These verses are encouraging; and though it is not the way we *feel* and *believe* some of the time; when the circumstances of life seem to clamp down on us—they are true!

If we are going to stabilize and truly reign in life, we need to understand that reigning in life is not the product of our performance [our plan]. We reign through our position, "in Christ!" So it is a matter of who we are, rather than what we do. In the Scripture above, the Holy Spirit through Paul made it clear, those who *receive* the *abundance of grace,* through Jesus Christ are the ones who reign in life (see Romans 8:13). Sin **shall not** be master over you, for you are not under law but *under grace.*

Legalism and Religious Christianity versus Grace

Many pastors and teachers avoid preaching and teaching true grace because they fear that to do so will give people the impression that **grace** provides occasion to sin rather than the liberty and peace promised in the Word of God. Therefore, they rationalize, it is much simpler to establish a set of stringent standards for rules, behavior and conduct rather than confuse **and lose** all of the people because of so-called grace to sin. This is clearly the nature of legalism. God forbid!

Webster's New Explorer Dictionary defines legalism as strict, literal, or excessive conformity to the law or to a religious or moral code, enforced.[11] Legalism always appeals to the flesh. Actually legalism has a first cousin named religion; which is also external and appealing to the flesh. So what I say about my topic, legalism applies to religious Christianity as well. It is impossible for the flesh to ever be able to produce the level of perfection God requires to be in union with Him.

Legalism and religious Christianity are great hindrances to true Christianity in that they concern themselves with those **external** things that are sensual [can be seen, smelled, heard, felt, or tasted]; for example by-laws, buildings, lifestyles, crowds and entertainment. They are clearly not listening to what the Spirit is saying to the churches (see Revelation 2:7). Jesus accused the Pharisees, the legalists and religionists of His day of:

- Equating the traditions of the elders with the sovereign will of God (see Matthew 15:2).
- "Teaching as doctrines the commandments of men" (Matthew 15:9).
- Making the commandments of God of no effect by their traditions (Matthew 15:6).

Today's Pharisees [legalists and religionists] have followed in the same tradition:

- The leaders in denominations have promoted democratic rule over biblical doctrine.
- They feel a threat to the status quo; therefore, they will in no way sanction the five ministers in Ephesians 4:11, who do not see themselves as subject to democratic processes.
- They oppose whatever they might perceive to be a threat to their doctrine of democratic ecclesiastical government.
- Since the year 2000, denominational leaders in the traditional church settings have begun to realize an accelerated decline not only in converts, but also the loss of many disillusioned truly born-again Christians from their rolls.
- True Spiritual Authority and unity are blocked in the Church by those promoting personal, religious Christianity and legalistic agendas through both no teaching and false

teaching which produces local churches with no Spirit (see Ephesians 4:11).

- Denominational constitutions and bylaws in many instances have created administrative positions that carry authority over the churches in a given locality.
- Pastors who do not happen to vote with the majority find themselves in trouble with the status quo [don't rock the boat].
- Like many other denominational church functions, voting is non-spiritual.

Fear of Change

A major reason that many leaders today do not want to hear what the Spirit is saying to the churches is fear. They are fearful because change threatens them and it pulls them out of their comfort zones. When legalists and religionists face change, they normally ask, "What is this going to cost me?" Someone has said, the seven last words of a dying church are, "We have never done it like that!"

Here we are more than a decade into the twenty-first century and many local traditional churches are up to the same form and same business as usual of the past century, sadly at a tremendous loss in:

- Spirituality
- Converts and Baptisms
- Commitments
- Church loyalty
- Generational discontinuity with those who are ages 18-29
- Families and individuals
- Civic and community support

Today very few people find legalism and religious Christianity desirable. Both require external participation through a series of laws. The same old set of laws, rules, and moral codes of conduct centered on what to eat, drink, hairstyles and how to dress. The truths of God's Word are neglected for science and reason. Because of the nature of today's religions, I do not classify true Christianity as a religion, but "the faith" a new biblical life and lifestyle. Because of the tremendously high percentage of spiritual and biblical ignorance many in the local churches easily compare with the Jews of Hebrews 5:12-14 who had:

- They had been exposed to the gospel of Christ, but were regressing in their understanding of the Messiah (v. 12).
- On milk when they should have been teachers on meat (v. 13).
- However, the writer declares, the one who comes to Christ for spiritual maturity is then **trained by the Word** to discern **truth** from **error** (v. 14).

People are realizing that they have been serving under an unscriptural parody of the real thing; and now they know there is more. Jesus invited unbelieving Jews and people everywhere to the salvation and maturity which only comes by **grace** through following Him in faith (see Matthew 19:21).

STUDY GUIDE: CHAPTER 3

1. _____ in our character and conduct draws people by the _____ of God to Christ in us. (PG. 35)

2. Through _____ _____ sin entered the world, and _____ through sin. (PG. 35)

3. Those who receive the _____ of grace and the _____ of will reign in life through the One, " _____ _____." (PG. 35)

4. We _____ through our _____ "in Christ." (PG. 36)

5. Legalism and _____ Christianity are extreme hindrances in that they concern themselves with _____ _____. (PG. 36)

6. What is the message to the churches recorded in Revelation 2:7? (PG. 36)

7. List several reasons why many church leaders do not want change: (PG. 37)
   1.
   2.
   3.

8. The person who comes to Christ for Spiritual maturity is trained by the _____ to _____ truth and error. (PG. 38)

CHAPTER 4

GRACELESS CHRISTIANITY

O foolish Galatians! Who has bewitched you that you should not obey the truth, before whose eyes Jesus Christ was clearly portrayed among you as crucified? This only I want to learn from you: **Did you receive the Spirit by the works of the law, or by the hearing of faith? Are you so foolish? Having begun in the Spirit, are you now being made perfect by the flesh?***"* (Galatians 3:1-3)

We've all probably heard the story of the famous football player asking a young boy, "When you grow up what man in the community would you like to be like?" The boy answered, "None!" Perhaps that question is by design, since in God's plan we are to be like Jesus Christ; which can only be accomplished through a personal knowing relationship with Him. However, this will not materialize until individual saints turn from following the Law and turn to Grace. As with the Galatians in the text above; beginning in the Spirit and then trying to go on to maturity in the flesh is the norm in too many local churches in America today.

In Hebrews 10:11-25 the writer says,

"And every priest stands ministering daily and offering repeatedly the same sacrifices, which can **never** *take away sins. But this Man, after He had offered one sacrifice for sins forever sat down at the right hand of God. Now where there is* **remission** *of these, there is no longer an offering for sin. "Therefore, brethren, having* **boldness** *to enter the Holiest by the blood of Jesus, by a* **new** *and* **living way** *which He consecrated for us, through the veil, that is His flesh, and having a High Priest over the house of God, let us draw near with a true heart in full assurance of faith, having our hearts sprinkled from an evil conscience and our bodies washed with pure water.* Emphasis added.

Full and final forgiveness has been achieved so that God does not remember sin anymore (v. 17); therefore no further sacrifice for sin is necessary. Notice, the narrow way:

- Faith in God leads believers to place their **hope** in the promises of God.
- Restored relationship with God encourages believers to restore their relationship with others (v. 23).
- Love for God manifests itself in love for others (v. 24).
- Assembling ourselves together, exhorting one another with truth as we see the Day of the Lord approaching (v. 25).
- Entrance into the Most Holy Place by a "new and living way"—through Jesus Christ's shed blood (vv. 19-22).
- No longer through the law, but now through **grace.**

The Divine Exchange

It doesn't take much reading in the gospels to meet the Pharisees. These keepers of the Law appointed themselves as the morality police. They prided themselves as more qualified to judge others and not themselves—as they claimed moral superiority as true followers of Judaism. They credited themselves with doing such a superior job at keeping God's laws that He had to be thoroughly impressed with them and totally disappointed with everyone else. However, Jesus shows us what really pleases God through His encounter with two immoral women. One, a Samaritan he met at a well (Study John 4:6-26) and the other was tossed down before Him as He taught a Bible study. She had been caught in the very act of adultery (Study John 8:2-11).

In both cases, Jesus extended **grace,** the Pharisees extended **condemnation** and **judgment.** We've all had encounters with self-righteous people just like these Pharisees. We can gather from both of these incidents that there are two very opposite kinds of righteousness:

- God-righteousness
- Self-righteousness

God Righteousness

God-righteousness comes from God; who is totally righteous. Everything He thinks, says, or does is exactly "right." Always God's righteousness is infinite, eternal and immutable. God is totally righteous because He is totally without sin. But, when it comes to people, *"All have sinned and fallen short of the glory of God"* (Romans 3:23). Because of sin, no man, woman, girl or boy can be righteous—*on their own.*

Only one upon whom God has conferred His own righteousness can be righteous. And that is exactly what He did! When Jesus took my place and died on the cross—*God* exchanged *my* sins for *His* righteousness. He was punished for my sins and I was credited for His righteousness:

"For He made Him who knew no sin to be sin for us, that we might become the righteousness of God in Him" (2 Corinthians 5:21).

Because Jesus was totally sinless, He was legally eligible to pay the penalty for all my sins [*past, present* and *future*]. Did you get that? [*past, present* and *future*] Praise God! God has legally declared me innocent! Not guilty! Righteous! Because of what Jesus did, I am now in "right standing" before God. He loves me and accepts me! All He asks for in return is my trust in His Son.

This same righteousness of Christ *"deposited to my account"* is available *free* to everyone who believes and receives Jesus Christ as their personal Savior. Christ volunteered and came down from heaven to take the punishment we deserved. We did absolutely nothing to deserve His love, Jesus died for us anyway. Christ is the giver of **grace** and we are the receivers. He reaches out to us— not us to Him. We can take absolutely no credit whatsoever for salvation. Grace is totally God's idea! It can't be worked for—nor can it be earned. It is a gift:

*"For it is by **grace** you have been saved, through faith, and that not of yourselves, it is the **gift** of God, **not** of works, lest anyone should boast"* (Ephesians 2:8-9). Emphasis is mine throughout.

47

For in it the righteousness of God is revealed from faith to faith as it is written, "The just shall live by faith"(Romans 1:17). Faith to faith means—God's grace through faith is at the beginning of the salvation process and it is the goal also. When a person first exercises this faith in Christ, that person is saved from the **penalty of sin and declared righteous.** As that person lives by God's **grace through faith,** God continues to save him or her from the **power of sin** to live righteously. True godly righteousness means desiring to live by God's truths of right and wrong and submitting to His leadership.

In his very fine article, What's Wrong with Grace, Mike Bickle defines the fruit of the biblical **grace** message as confidence in the **gift** of God's **love** combined with a spirit of **obedience.**[12]

Bickle makes another point that I think is very important to counter the many negative assertions of skeptics and those who are afraid to preach and teach biblical grace. They think it gives an approving nod toward sin. *"If either of these two elements love or obedience is missing, then it isn't the true message."*[13] This truth as with so many other truths of God's Word was lost during the Dark Ages, (391-1517). The people had to believe what they were told, because the Bible was not written in their language and not available to the people. Today the doctrine of true biblical grace is reemerging in the churches as the day approaches for Christ to return for His Bride (see Revelation 19:7).

Self-righteousness
Ever since Adam and Eve had their Garden experience with Satan, human beings have tried to establish and live by their own **sensual** truth and standards of *righteousness*—morally independent of God. Certainly this was Lucifer's downfall:

How you are fallen from heaven, O Lucifer, son of the morning!
How you are cut down to the ground,
You who weakened the nations!
For you have said in your heart:
I will ascend into heaven,
I will exalt my throne
Above the stars of God;
I will also sit on the mount
Of the congregation

> *I will ascend above the heights of the clouds*
> *I will be like the Most High;*
> (Isaiah 14:12-14).

Lucifer [Satan] told Adam and Eve they too could be like the Most High, doing their own thing: *"When you eat of it your eyes will be opened, and you will be like God, knowing good and evil"* (Genesis 3:5) NIV. They fell for it and we've been a fallen world ever since. Down through the generations that followed we see the depravity as the results of "self-redemption;" which in Noah's day led to God sending the flood to wipe them out (see Genesis 7-8).

But Noah found **grace** in the eyes of the Lord (Genesis 6:8). Think about it, had there not been a man and a family **who by God's grace stood** from the wickedness of their day; God would have had a new day without humanity. After the flood, Noah and his family repopulated the earth with a people more wicked and degenerate than those before the flood.

Then came the Law
After the Law of Moses was given, every attempt to obey it failed. Though some people did better than others at keeping the law, nobody completely obeyed it. From the high priest to the lowly shepherd, nobody made a perfect score of 100%. Jesus came to the lowly because they knew they needed help. However, those with much, many times don't think they need a Savior. Instead of asking for mercy or help the self-righteous person will simply work harder, shout more, sing louder or pray longer.

The Law fails the best of us—Grace saves the worst of us!

When a self-righteous person is caught wrong or they fall short in a matter, they explain it away. "At least, I'm not as bad as so and so." They set their own standards and scores:

"Those who live according to the flesh set their minds on the things of the flesh, but those who live according to the Spirit, the things of the Spirit" (Romans 8:5).

When the subject of *legalism* comes up the question, "How can I ignore his or her sins or faulty behavior?" Is that Christian? The answer is yes and no. Salvation under legalism brings converts to the church itself and not to Christ. Therefore, what these individuals will receive is advice [advice has no saving power] pertaining to some aspect of the church's constitution and by-laws based on **performance of works** not **biblical grace.**

Many Christians today, including many pastors, still have not died to their legalistic attitudes. These people hold certain standards for the Gospel, depending on the denomination that they think meet terms for God's acceptance. These standards are weighted down with manmade rules. In his Epistle to the Colossians the apostle Paul warned about "Don't touch that, don't eat this, wear this type of clothing, and don't wear lip stick or jewelry." Many people remain under these **doctrines of works** thinking that they make them holy. They hear the truths of God's word, but reject it because they won't accept the fact that their beliefs are in error. So when the truth is preached and they hear it, they become very offended and cry foul! "You don't believe in holiness; and have moved to teaching permissiveness."

Grace versus Law

The Galatian believers were under pressure from Jewish legalists and were considering rejection of the gospel of grace and reverting back to dependence on the Mosaic Law for salvation. Paul writing this letter to the Galatians was the outline for the many differences between these two approaches to God:[14]

Grace	**Law**
Is based in **faith** (2:16)	Is based on **works** (2:16)
Justifies sinful men [and women] (2:16-17)	Is incapable of justification (2:16; 3:11)

Begins and ends with Christ (2:20)	Makes Christ nothing (5:2)
Is the way of the **Spirit** (3:2; 3, 14)	Is the way of the **flesh** (3:3)
Is a "blessing" (3:14)	Is a "curse" (3:13)
Is God's desired end for His people (3:23, 25)	Intended to be a means to an end (3:23)
Results in intimacy with Christ (3:27)	Estrangement from Christ (5:4)
Makes one a son of God and an heir of Christ (4:6, 7)	keeps one a slave (4:7)
Brings liberty (5:1)	Results in bondage (5:1)
Depends on the power of the Holy Spirit (5:16-18, 22, 23)	Depends on human effort (5:19-21)
Is motivated by love (5:13, 14)	Is motivated by pride (6:3, 13, 14)
Centers on the cross of Christ (6:13-14)	Centers on circumcision (5:11, 6:12-15)

We are saved by grace through faith. The Pharisees like many members in the local church, failed to grasp the fact that redemption come before righteousness. And you cannot redeem yourself. Therefore, anyone who thinks they can become righteous by *performance of works* is in error. Paul said, *"For if righteousness could be gained through the law, Christ died for nothing"* (Galatians 2:21). Any counsel the believer passes to someone must be by the Spirit, biblically-based and showered upon with love and grace.

Leading people to Jesus is our job—transforming their lives is His job.

Our task is leading people to Christ. However, many get confused and think we also are responsible for transformation in others [God's job]. Only one person is holy, Jesus Christ; therefore, all of our holiness must come by grace accessed by faith in Him.

Performance of works negates biblical grace.

STUDY GUIDE: CHAPTER 4

1. Too many local churches begin in the _____, but try to go on to _____ in the _____. (PG. 40).

2. On what basis is there no longer further sacrifices _____ _____ necessary? (PG. 40)

3. Entrance into the most holy place by a "_____ _____ _____" through the _____ of Jesus. (PG 40)

4. There are two kinds of righteousness, _____ righteousness and _____ righteousness. (PG. 41)

5. No one can be righteous on their _____. (PG. 41)

6. Christ saved us from the _____ of sin. (PG. 42)

7. The message of biblical grace includes the two elements of _____ and _____. (PG. 42)

8. Noah found _____ in the sight of the Lord. (PG. 43).

9. Many today rely on _____ of works as opposed to _____ _____. (PG. 43)

SECTION II

GRACE IS AMAZING

CHAPTER 5

WHAT KIND OF PEOPLE ARE WE [TO BE?]

Baptized into one body [unity] describes the people of God who in the knowledge of the Son of God, grow to a perfect man and fullness of Christ. This must be the goal of every Church (see Ephesians 4:11-14). Satan expertly projects mainly through his infiltrated children, a united oneness based on **sensual** perception [received from the five senses] void of biblical grace. Therefore, their perception of an example would have to be some athlete, Hollywood star, or other famous world figure most of whom have never met Christ.[15]

A perfect man, being all that God intended, Christ was totally dependent on the Father, for all He was, for all He said, and for all He did. He is the perfect *example* for **all believers** to follow. The apostle Peter declares that Christ *"left us an example that we should follow in His steps"* (1 Peter 2:21).[16] What then is the example set forth for the man or woman of **grace** in Christ's perfect Manhood?

Jesus is our Example in Character

The moral character and qualities of God were manifested in Jesus Christ as the Perfect Man. These same moral attributes are to be manifested through **grace** in the believer also; as he or she is transformed into the image of Christ. Christ's example is manifest through *grace* in the mature believer:

Holiness
Jesus is our Example in holiness. He is holy in nature and conduct. Peter admonishes, *"But as He who called you is holy, you also be holy in all your conduct, because it is written, "Be holy for I am holy."* He is our example of sinless perfection and it is to this goal that God intends to ultimately bring His people (Study: Matthew 5:48; Hebrews 6:1; Luke 1:35; Acts 2:37; 3:14; 4:27; Hebrews 4:15; 7:26; 1 Peter 2:21-23; John 8:29, 46; 14:30).[17]

The person committed to God's holiness says, No! To fleshly lusts and lives in obedience to the will of God. The holy person is always alert, keeping his or her mind clear and fit for their walk with God. Be honest, sincere, and pure in all your relationships. Love one another fervently!

Love

I stated earlier, Christ is our Example in love; which is the very nature of God manifested in the saints. *To know the love of Christ which passes knowledge; that you may be filled with all the fullness of God* (Ephesians 3:19):

- He loved the Father (John 14:31; 6:38).
- He loved the Scriptures (Matthew 5:17-18; Luke 4:16-21; 24:44-45; John 10:34-36).
- He loved His own disciples (John 13:1; 15:9; Romans 8:37-39).
- He loves the Church as His own Bride (Ephesians 5:25-27).
- He loves all men regardless of race (Mark 10:21; Matthew 11:19; John 10:11; 15:13; Romans 5:8).
- He loved His enemies (Matthew 5:43-48; Luke 22:51; 23:34; Matthew 26:50).
- He prayed that this love would be in us (John 17:26; 13:34-35).
- He was continually moved with compassion towards others (John 11:35; 6:5; Mark 6:34; Matthew 8:16; 20:34; Luke 4:41; 5:12-15).

Humility

Christ is our example in humility. No pride, no harshness, nor arrogance ever manifested themselves in Him. In the gospel of John, Jesus' life becomes open to us. He frequently speaks of:

- His relationship with the Father.
- The motives by which He was guided.
- His consciousness of the Spirit and power in which He acts.

Though in the word humility, humble is not written, His humility is clearly revealed. Humility defined is nothing but the Christian simply consenting to let God be all, and he or she surrendering totally to His will alone.

Humility through *grace* is true humility, for it puts all believers on the same footing. For we all have come short of His glory. Had it not been for His grace [unmerited favor] all of us would be lost to the lake of fire. Because of grace, nobody can look down upon another in judgment or pride of attainment. The ground is level at the cross.

His humility is to be manifested through us. What He taught often was true of Him: *He who humbles himself will be exalted* (Luke 18:4). As it is written," *He humbled Himself wherefore God also has highly exalted Him"* (Philippians 2:8-9). We are further told that we are to manifest Christ's attitude of meekness, unselfishness, servanthood, obedience and to let the mind of Christ be in us (see Philippians 2:5-8; Matthew 1:28-30; II Corinthians 10:1).

Unlike the self-righteous Pharisees, who thought themselves greater than all men, as God's chosen defenders? They lived a phony religious life, pretending they had no need of forgiveness. When Christ speaks of His relationship with the Father, He uses the words *not* and *nothing,* of Himself:

1. *"The Son can do **nothing** of Himself"* (John 5:19).
2. *"I can of My own self do **nothing**; My judgment is just, because I do **not** seek My own will"* (John 5:30).
3. *"Neither came I Myself, but He sent Me"* (John 8:42).
4. *"The words I speak unto you, I speak **not** from Myself"* (John 14:10).
5. *"The word which you hear is **not** Mine but the Father's who sent Me"* (John 14:24).

These words tell us how the Almighty God was able to work His mighty redemptive plan through Christ. His humility is to be manifested to the world through us. He was able to humble Himself before men also; no matter what men might say of Him or do to Him. This is true self-denial to which our Savior calls us, the acknowledgment that *self has nothing good in it except as an empty vessel which God must fill.*

Jesus teaches us that true humility finds its strength in the knowledge that it is God who through **grace** works all in all, that our place is to yield to Him in perfect resignation and dependence—in full consent to be and do nothing of ourselves. This is the life Christ came to manifest and impart to us, a life in Christ that comes through death to sin and self. If while we were yet the enemies we were reconciled to God through the death of His Son, much more shall we be saved by His life (Romans 5:10). If Christ was able to reconcile us through His death; certainly He can keep us by His resurrection power.

The Scriptures says, *"Or do you not know that as many of us as were baptized into His death? Likewise you also reckon yourselves to be dead indeed to sin, but alive to God in Christ Jesus, our Lord. And do not present your members as instruments of unrighteousness to sin, but present yourselves to God as being alive from the dead, and your members as instruments of righteousness to God"* (Romans 6:3, 11, 13). Christ lives this life by grace in us through His indwelling Spirit!

STUDY GUIDE: CHAPTER 5

1. Baptized into the _____ _____
    describes the people of God. (PG. 47)

2. Christ was totally _____ on the Father for all He
    was _____ _____ _____ and
    _____ _____ _____ (PG. 47)

3. The moral _____ of God was _____ in
    Jesus Christ. (PG 47)

4. The person committed to God's _____ says
    _____ to fleshly _____ and lives in obedience
    to _____ _____ _____
    _____. (PG. 47)

5. Humility is to be _____ through us. (PG. 48)

6. When Christ speaks of His relationship with the Father, He uses
    the words _____ and _____ of Himself. (PG. 48)

7. Jesus teaches that true _____ finds its
    strength in the _____ that it is God of through
    _____ works all in all. (PG. 49)

8. Christ lives the life of _____ through us. (PG. 49)

CHAPTER 6

LIVING GRACE

For You, O Lord, will bless the righteous;
*with **favor** You will surround him as with a shield*
(Psalm 5:12).

For the Lord God is a sun and shield;
*The Lord will give **grace** and glory;*
No good thing will He withhold
From those who walk uprightly.
(Psalm 84:11)

Within the past decade, this nation has witnessed what many claim to be more than our share of disasters. Many in Christian leadership have determined that these events were the result of God's wrath for one reason or another. After Haiti's devastating earthquake in 2010, among many prophetic leaders, one prominent TV Evangelist stood out as he stepped forth and declared that God had judged the already poverty-stricken country for its spiritual ties with witchcraft. Many voiced the same for New Orleans after the Katrina disaster. The devastating fires and flooding in Colorado kept the nation on edge for days.

Last year the news media spoke of the heaviest snowfall in South Dakota's history, at the same time, a major fire on the west coast, and devastating tornados in the plains States which were predicted to cause damage all the way to the east coast. At the same time the remnants of a tropical storm moved up the east coast causing a loss of lives, widespread flooding, downed trees, power outages, and devastated Jersey shore. Certainly to blame God's wrath is a misrepresentation of the most damaging kind.

Additionally, we all probably remember the preacher a couple of years ago who predicted the world would come to an end on a certain date. The date came and went and the end did not come. He made adjustments for a later date; this time was different due to national publicity. The media broadcasted the event worldwide paying particular attention to some of this preacher's followers, who sold their homes, quite their jobs—and it did not come to past. What a witness before the world! We are continually challenged and confused by our limited understanding of how God's grace and wrath work in tandem, and what it means in a world facing the consequences of its own sinful nature.

The idea of judgment and disaster being the result of sin was around when Jesus walked upon the earth. In Luke 13:4, He addressed this when referring to the eighteen on whom the tower in Siloam fell and killed. In His answer to whether disaster proves God's wrath, Jesus asked, *"Do you suppose that these Galileans were worse sinners than all other Galileans, because they suffered such things?" I tell you, no; but **unless you repent** you will likewise perish"* (vv. 4-5). Jesus indicated that the **real issue** is not judgment **but repentance.** [Emphasis added throughout] Likewise America, "we need to repent!" While such a view was common then among the Jews it was **not always** a correct conclusion (Study Exodus 20:5; Job 4:7, 8:4. 20; 22:5; Proverbs 10:24, 25; John 9:1-3). Jesus is pointing to the fact that all of us are only a step away from death until repentance comes. This was a natural tragedy as opposed to violent human act of Pilate's mingling Galileans blood with the sacrifice alluded to in (vv. 1-2). However, the same question was asked here. Were the people who suffered death being judged for their sins? Again, Jesus answers, *"No, but unless you repent you will **all** likewise perish"* (v. 5). The manner in which a person dies **is not** a measure of righteousness; what is important is **not to die** outside of **God's grace.**

"I have not come to call the righteous, but sinners, to repentance."
—Jesus Christ

The way to prevent that from happening is to **repent,** and come to God through the **grace** of the Great Physician, Jesus Christ. Jesus' mission was to call sinners to **repentance** (Luke 5:32). He commissioned His disciples **to the same task.** A humble approach to God for spiritual healing is the essence of repentance.

The Scribes and Pharisees are always present

Many Christians individually and corporately are perfectly satisfied in separating themselves totally from the company of sinners. The Scribes and Pharisees are still with us today and still up to their old self-righteousness and prejudices. Jesus stated that He did not come to the righteous [in this case the Pharisees and Scribes] who felt they had no need of **spiritual healing.** In essence He was saying that only those who **know** their spiritual need can be treated. Like these Pharisees and Scribes, so many self-righteous people in our churches will not come for aid, and in their own eyes—do not need a doctor.

As our Example, Jesus modeled the proper attitude toward sinners and how we should interact with them. By His sitting down and eating with such company, the Scribes and Pharisees believed then and those sharing such attitude today believe that such behavior on His part conveyed an acceptance of the person's sin. Jesus preferred pursuing **relationships** that might lead sinners to God rather than "quarantining" Himself from such people.

In his book, "Preaching to a Post Modern World," Graham Johnson says, "Too often today individuals and churches can consciously or unconsciously promote an elitist mentality that those inside the church are the "good people." It is also easy to convey the idea that those outside are "bad people" so we are to bring them in and make good people of them."[18]

Romans 3:23 says, **"All have sinned and [all] fall short of the glory of God."** That is a humbling, but encouraging verse of Scripture. God revealed to people how they should live, *but no one can live up to God's perfect way.* We cannot save ourselves because as sinners we can never meet God's requirements. Our only hope is **grace through faith in Jesus Christ and His death.** Paul gives two reasons why the righteousness of God comes only through Christ's death:

- First, it demonstrates that God Himself is righteous, and did not judge the sins committed prior to the cross.
- Second, by it God wanted to show that He is both righteous and at the same time the **One** who can declare sinner's righteous.

Because of Christ's death, God does not compromise His holiness when He forgives a sinner. God is the **only One** righteous, and for that reason we should praise Him! He deserves our highest praise!

If Christ ate with sinners to reconcile them back to God—we are to do likewise. We should help the postmodern people to humbly accept the nature of **grace.** When we proclaim or hear this message of grace proclaimed, no one can claim superiority before God and *no one is excluded from the invitation into God's presence!*

In truth, **grace is risky.** I love it because we all must begin with humility. While here on the earth the Bible says, "Jesus humbled Himself and became obedient unto death" (Philippians 2:8). In his book Humility, Andrew Murray says, "Christ's humility gave value to His death and so He became our redemption." Further, our relationship with God and fellow human beings must be marked by an all pervading humility.[19] Without humility there can be no true abiding in God's presence or any experience of His **grace** and **power** of His **Spirit.** This teaching and example has been **neglected** in the churches probably because of fear from a false perception of grace which without revival will continue. God forbid!

Murray defines humility as the sense of entire nothingness, which comes when we see how truly God is all, and in which we make way for God to be all. We must realize that this is **true grace** and must consent to be, with our will, mind and affections, the form and the vessel in which the life and glory of God are to work and manifest themselves.[20] To live this life of total dependency by grace through faith, Jesus Christ Himself will give us this grace as a part of His wonderful life within us.

In "The Knowledge of the Holy" A.W. Tozer explains, "Grace is the good pleasure of God that inclines Him to bestow benefits upon the undeserving. It is a self-existent principle inherent in the divine nature and appears to us as a self-caused propensity to pity the wretched, spare the guilty, welcome the outcast, and bring into favor those who were before under just disapprobation. Its use to us sinful men [and women, boys and girls] is to save us and make us sit together in heavenly places to demonstrate to the ages the exceeding riches of God's kindness to us in Christ Jesus."[21]

Be Real [Authentic]

Community grows out of authenticity of living grace which frees every person to be real. Yet authenticity in churches must begin in the pulpit and permeate throughout the congregation. The leadership will promote either depth or shallowness. The lack of authenticity stands out as one of the **major** reasons people cite for leaving the church. In Preaching to a Postmodern World, Graham Johnson cites a quote from William Hendricks, "There seems to be a feeling that religious situations too often lack authenticity. The truth is not told; people are not "real.' Christian sermons, books, and conversations to often seemed to avoid the "bad stuff.'"

Indeed, religion sometimes seems off in a world of its own. Yet my interviews felt that if faith is to make any difference in people's lives, it has to face cold, hard reality. It also has to get under the surface to a person's real self, to one' sin, and pain and the things one wants to hide.[22]

Johnson also cites Calvin Miller and affirms the biblical message must be presented:

- In relation to the lives of the people.
- In relation to the life of the speaker.
- Through a relational, casual approach that willingly allows people to get close and in getting close, they'll sense a heart that beats for God and community will form as people are willing to be vulnerable with one another about their victories and struggles.
- I recall hearing the story of a pastor who sat through an AA meeting and one man stood and rejoiced over not taking a drink during a designated period and he was loudly applauded for his victory. A woman stood and began to speak of her failure admitting to taking a drink during the designated period. The group applauded and confirmed this lady with the same enthusiasm as the victorious man before. The pastor left in tears as he thought of the different way people are handled in church. How does your church handle sin-sick people?
- But this authenticity must start at the top.[23]

Issues like sexuality and sexual conduct, managing finances, growing relationships, and prioritizing one's life are in the forefront of people's minds. People want to know if the truths of God's Word [the Bible] can stand up to modern pressures in their lives; we must assure them—it can and will! In our counsel we must speak the truth in love.

Through Grace

Grace and mercy together in action are beautiful. However, people cannot fathom God's idea of grace because it doesn't make sense to them. Tozer declares that in God grace and mercy are one; but as they reach us today are seen as two, related but not identical. As mercy is God's goodness confronting human misery and guilt, so grace is His goodness directed toward human debt and demerit. It is by His grace that God imputes merit where none previously existed and declares no debt to be where one had been before.[24] The parable in Matthew 20 illustrates both thoughts:

- God's **grace** rewards each worker with equal pay, regardless of time and effort.
- Human thinking says, the persons who worked longer should receive a greater paycheck.

The apostle Paul, who far beyond all others is the exponent of grace in redemption, never disassociates God's grace from God's crucified Son. Always in his teachings the two are found together, one and inseparable. In Ephesians 1:4-6, he offers this summary:

*". . . . Having predestined us to adoption as sons by Jesus Christ Himself, according to the riches of His will, to the praise of the glory of His grace, by which He made us accepted in the Beloved. In Him we have redemption through His blood, the forgiveness of sins, according to the riches of **His grace** . . . ."*

Through the shedding of His precious blood, Christ bought us from our slavery to sin. The blood of Christ is the means by which our redemption comes. Both the Old and New Testaments clearly teach that there is no forgiveness of sin without the shedding of blood.

STUDY GUIDE: CHAPTER 6

1. Is the devastation America is presently experiencing due to the _____ of God? PG. 51

2. God's _____ and _____ works in tandem. PG. 51

3. Jesus indicated that the real issue is not judgment but _____ PG. 51

4. Individuals and churches can promote an elitist _____ that those outside are _____ PG. 52

5. Our relationship with God and fellow human beings must be marked by _____ _____ _____ PG. 53

6. In truth _____ is risky. PG. 53

7. _____ stands out as one of the major reasons people are leaving the _____ PG. 53

Explain the blood of Jesus in salvation:

CHAPTER 7

CHURCH AND GRACE REDEFINED

"And I also say unto you that you are Peter,
and on this rock
I will build My church,
and
the gates of Hades shall not prevail
against it."
(Matthew 16:20)

What happened to the church that Jesus began? Can you find it? Is the divided Christianity we see around us that church? Jesus not only promised He would build His church. He also assured His disciples that the gates of hell would not prevail against it. How can you find His church today?

By the end of the third century the true servants of God had become a distinct minority among those who called themselves Christianity. The religious Christianity became the majority. Millions of people professed Christianity and claimed to be members of the Church of Jesus Christ.

Christianity is divided into denominations and schisms; which have assimilated many non-biblical traditions, philosophical, cultural and religious errors into their teachings and practices. Can we know whether Christianity's bewildering variety of customs and teachings in our local churches faithfully represent those of Jesus Christ? Only the truth of God's Word [the Bible] can provide reliable answers to these questions.

Saints and Ain'ts

The true biblical church is—those people [saints] called of God to follow Jesus. When Christianity became the National religion of the Roman Empire under Constantine in A.D. 325 many soul-saving biblical truths were lost as the religious Christianity or *[ain'ts]* came into the church in droves under the Emperor's proclamation. In the

69

Reformation [a Mighty move of God] began in A.D. 1517; using a Roman Catholic priest named Martin Luther as His lightning rod, God restored many of the lost biblical truths of His Word. God has used other saints since then and more truths have been restored and are being restored to this day in A.D. 2014. The Spirit of God is revealing these truths of God's Word **afresh** to those churches *[saints]* who are **hearing what the Spirit is saying**; which requires a heart for God. Let me clarify, this is not a new revelation! Jesus commanded the churches to: *"Hear what the Spirit says to the churches"* (see Revelation 2:7).

Across this nation more and more people are claiming that they are not being Spiritually-fed in their local churches. Until a radical determination for the teaching of the truths of God's Word and a biblical worldview, is realized in the churches; this spiritual hunger will continue to go unmet and we will find our people going [not to other denominations or even non-denominational] within Christianity, but also to other faith groups. This fault lies at the feet of the spiritual leadership. We are servants of the Word of God and certainly—we should have the truth to feed our people. Advice may help in some situations [religious Christianity is full of rational advice] but the Bible says it's the truth that sets you free [only true Christianity imparts the truths of God's Word!].

The Age of Grace

For the past two thousand years, humanity has lived [admitted or not] in what is called the Age of Grace and/or the Church Age. On the cross Jesus shouted, "It is finished" meaning the work the Father sent Him to accomplish was completed. What was that work? He shed His blood and died a sacrificial death for the sins of the whole world. That is the epitome of **grace.** The Scripture says, "While we were yet sinners Christ died for the ungodly [us]" (Study Romans 5:6-21). Grace abounded, praise God!

Stated earlier, Adam put humanity into a depraved state that only God could get us out of. The Bible says, the life of the flesh is in the blood (see Leviticus 17:11). When Adam sinned in the garden his blood became corrupted and his flesh sinful. Though God continued to speak audible to humans, they were cut-off from God's presence who is holy.

No more walks in the cool of the evening with God for Adam and Eve. They were alienated from God, a state which they passed on to their off springs. They lost their home [the Garden of Eden] and now homeless they had to till the ground for sustenance. Let' look at grace:

- By grace God drove them from the Garden, had they ate from the tree of life in their sinful state [sin within them would have perpetuated] (see Genesis 3:24).
- By grace God killed two animals [shed blood] and in His mercy made tunics to cover Adam and Eve's nakedness (see Genesis 3:21).
- By grace God promised (see Genesis 3:15) the coming One whom we know to be the Lord Jesus, the Messiah who would bruise Satan's head. Satan would bruise His heel, that is, He suffered a terrible but temporary injury [death] (see John 12:32; Colossians 2:15). By grace in His resurrection, Christ defeated His enemy. (Study Romans 6-8).

The Great Commandment

Everything God requires of His people and every tenet of right living in the Bible are founded on two principles in the Great Commandment (see Matthew 22:37-40:

- "Love the Lord your God with all your heart and with all soul and with all your mind" (v. 37). ***"O magnify the Lord with me and let us exalt His name together"*** (Psalm 34:3).

WORSHIPPING GOD IS THE CHURCH'S FIRST PURPOSE!

- "Love your neighbor as yourself. All the Law and the Prophets hang on these two commandments (vv. 38-39).
  Love for neighbors [ministry] id demonstrating God's love to others by meeting their needs and healing their hurts in the name of Jesus. The church is to equip the saints to carry out this task (see Ephesians 4:11-12).

Though the churches have their marching orders from Christ Himself; little true ministry is taking place in many of our local churches.

One day Jesus was asked to identify the most important commandment. He condensed all the Law and the Prophets into the two tasks above (see v. 40). Jesus also gave His disciples the Great Commission for bringing people into God's eternal family I believe that every church can be validated by their obedience to Christ's Great Commandment and Great Commission.

The church includes all of those called to follow Jesus. One day each of us will give an account to God regarding our faithfulness and obedience to these commands!

The Great Commission #1

*"Then the eleven disciples went away into Galilee, to the mountain which Jesus had appointed for them. When they **saw Him,** they worshipped Him . . . ." And **Jesus came** and spoke to them saying, "All authority has been given to Me in heaven and on earth"* (Matthew 28:16-18).

Later in His last words to His disciples, Jesus gave His disciples the Great Commission; which actually **consists of five Great Commissions.** In his book the *Purpose Driven Church*, Rick Warren explains, "in the Greek text of the Great Commission there are three present participle verbs: *going, baptizing,* and *teaching.* Each of these is a part of the command to "make disciples." **Going, baptizing** and **teaching** are the essential elements of the disciple-making process.[25]

*"**Go** and **make disciples** of all nations, **baptizing them** in the name of the Father and of the Son and of the Holy Spirit, and **teaching them** to obey everything I have commanded you"* (Matthew 28:19-20). Emphasis is mine.

Great Commission #2

Later Jesus appeared to the eleven. And He said to them, *"Go into all the world and preach the gospel to every creature"* (Mark 16:15).

Great Commission #3

Jesus said to His disciples, *"And that repentance and remission of sins be preached in His name to all nations, beginning at Jerusalem. And you are witnesses of these things. Behold I send the **promise** of My Father upon you; but tarry in the city of Jerusalem until you are endued with power from on high"* (Luke 24:47-49).

Great Commission #4

So Jesus said to them again, *"Peace to you! As the Father has sent Me, I also send you"* (John 20:21).

Great Commission #5

"But you shall receive power when the Holy Spirit has come upon you and you shall be witnesses to Me in Jerusalem, and in Judea and Samaria, and to the end of the earth" (acts 1:8).

The Great Commandment when combined with the Great Commission establishes a clear picture of God's plan through Scriptural, supernatural commitments for the Body of Christ in the world:

- Love God with all your heart (Matthew 22:37-40).
- Love your neighbor as yourself (Matthew 22:37-40).
- Make Disciples (Matthew 28:19-20).
- Preach the gospel to every creature (Mark 16:15).
- Preach repentance and remission of sins (Luke 24:47-49).
- Be sent by Jesus (John 29:21).
- **[Wait!]** Be empowered by the Holy Spirit (Acts 1:8).

Unfortunately, very little actual ministry is being accomplished by the local churches; because many have abandoned both the

Great Commandments and the Great Commissions either as not relevant or impossible in their *natural* abilities. These churches search for and create their own forms of godliness (see 2 Timothy 3:5) to fill the now non-spiritual void in the absence of the [Holy Spirit's direction, guidance and power]. They adapt community programs and activities [many from secular resources] for their own entertainment rather than true worship. Others simply conform to the secular and immorally-charged culture around them. To do this is willful disobedience and open rebellion in the face of Christ's purpose and mission for the church in the world; which He personally assigned. God forbid!

During my pastoral ministry, one difficulty for me was to keep people fully engaged in the churches' ministries once their children have grown up and left home. I am not talking about novices per se, but many supposedly mature Christians. The same behavior seems to accompany the life of pastors once they relinquish the pastoral ministry. Some retire to a life of travel, fishing for *bass* or another favorite hobby. Once we are called of God to be servants of the Word of God, there can be no retirement per se. If that had been the Apostle John's attitude we probably would not know the future world events as recorded in the Book of Revelation nor would we have the wonderful treasures of John's Pastoral Epistles [I-III John] all recorded in his nineties.

Watch the news and you will see that every major network has secured the expertise of retired Military Generals and Admirals along with their retired civilian counterparts. Their task is to interpret the times and world events as expert news annalists for the networks. When God's Generals go silent who is going to speak into the generations? Who is going to launch the new wineskins? Who is going to keep the true biblical worldview and early church foundation sound and shored up?

Picture with me two of God's Old Testament Prophets, notice as Isaiah preached we are given a picture of the people standing there with their fingers in their ears—he did not quite! Then there was John the Baptist preaching out in the hot, dry uncomfortable desert with its snakes and other critters—but the people came in droves to hear that voice crying in the wilderness. Only death would stop him! We've also had great experiences in the Lord, during our Holy Spirit directed supernatural ministries. God still has a work for us to do. Like Paul our spirits are renewed and therefore teachable every day!

Anointed Wineskins

The Holy Spirit has been taking the true church of God through a restoration process in conjunction with God's over all redemption plan. He is placing the saints back into their rightful places of kings and priests. While the world is going about trying every thing they can to remove Jesus' name from the public square; God is raising up kings to go forth throughout the marketplace to lift Jesus up and extend His kingdom. Of course the priests' charge is the House of God in shepherding the people of God and equipping them to carry out the Great Commission.

People love their familiar comfort zones in the church and marketplace; which give rise to resistance to change. There is an old saying, "If it's not broke don't fix it." So they are afraid of anyone who begin to talk about changing what they have been use to all their lives. As a result of sin in the world, many errors and counterfeit truths are being propagated in the local churches as more and more people of the secular persuasion find their way into the congregations. Unless the local churches remain alert, relevant, teachable, and flexible for change through Spiritual and biblical transformation—they will be as salt which has lost its savor. God prepares and uses anointed new wineskins to contain and affect necessary change [new wine] as they receive [hear] what the Spirit is saying to the churches.

To make a wineskin new, God soaks the old wineskin in water (the Word of God) and rubs in the oil (the Holy Spirit); but that oil also contains a new anointing. In this restorative process, God takes what was there and brings it to a new place so that He can pour within it that which He longs to release, new wine to His people. The Prophet Isaiah particularly and others prophesied concerning the coming of the New Wine, Jesus Christ and John the Baptist launched the New Wine. As we allow the Holy Spirit to take us through the process of rubbing we not only become more pliable and flexible, but we can handle all that God desires to pour into us, and we are able to pour out in greater measure.[26]

The Holy Spirit took my wife and I through the restorative process from old to new wineskins. In 1998 we founded the Bread of Life Bible Ministries with the mission of pouring the new wine of the *restored truths of God's Word*; truths that had once guided the church, but lost during the Dark Ages of the true church (see Jude 3). For the past fifteen years we have been pouring the truth of God's Word into the saints producing mature disciples who go forth throughout the church and marketplace with their biblical worldview, and the truths of God's Word in turn pouring out to others who in turn does the same (see 2 Timothy 2:2).

I mentioned in an earlier section that in 1998 when we began the Bread of Life Bible Institute, the Barna Group reported 20 Million Christians who no longer attended the institutional or traditional churches. According to recent Barna research that figure has increased to 115 million over the last fifteen years. Many of these people are leaving the local churches because many churches have left their first love, [Christ] and have ceased pursuing His established purposes, the Great Commandments and the Great Commission.

Unanointed Wineskins

Most denominations were established on the premise that democratic rule needed to be incorporated into their legal structure. It is important to note that the introduction of democracy into church government came from the *culture* of the time rather than the Word of God. A check of church history reveals that most denominations were *originally* founded by apostles even though the term was seldom used. The process of authority over time shifted from the individual to a group. Group rule was sealed with denominational constitutions and bylaws. Individual leaders were kept in line through denominational dictates by various established systems of *legal* checks and balances.

The unanointed of religious Christianity rose up in the denominations among the power brokers. These old wineskins demonically work behind the scenes almost impossible to detect. Their goal is to preserve the status quo of the old wineskin, and through legalism and religion hinder or stop the new wineskin's move into *God's new times* and *seasons*. Their works are the same today as in the days of their counterpart, the Pharisees who equated the traditions of the fathers with the sovereign will of God. They asked Jesus, "Why do your disciples transgress the *traditions of the fathers?"*(see Matthew 15:2). In response Jesus used tough language. He accused them of *"teaching as doctrines the commandments of men"* (Matthew 15:9). Jesus also said, *"You have made the commandment of God of no effect by your tradition"* (Matthew 15:6). The Pharisees clearly were not hearing what the Spirit was then saying to the churches (see Revelation 2:7). That same unanointed spirit roams rampart among the churches' leadership today.

The Holy Spirit began to breathe change a [new wineskin] into the denominations first mentioned by John Wesley as a warm feeling during his preaching. Eventually this move of the Spirit restored consecration and sanctification to the body of Christ.

One of the traditions of the elders in denominations that countered the Holy Spirit's move and continues to hinder His work is that *democratic rule* has over time become a de facto doctrine. A major threat to the status quo has been the introduction of the *restored* New Testament Church; which recognizes *all* the ministers of Ephesians 4:11 exercising giftedness in the leadership. These ministers do not see themselves as subject to *democratic processes.* It should come as no surprise, then, that denominational leaders would oppose whatever comes that may be considered a threat to *their* doctrine of democratic government.

State Churches
While there were some free churches in the territories, beginning with the Protestant Reformation, the non-Roman Catholic state churches were the new wineskin and by the grace of God several lost truths of God's Word were restored:

- Eternal life
- The translation of the Bible from Latin to the vernacular of the people.
- The doctrine of the priesthood of all believers.
- The just shall live by faith.

Restoration of these graces tremendously changed the nature of church life. When state churches became the old wineskin, the new wineskin that emerged was denominations formed in America.[27]

Denominations

As denominations move to old wineskin status, we must remember that they were at one time the new wineskins. God poured His new wine into them, and used the denominational structure mightily to:

- Spread the gospel around the world.
- Denominational structure.
- Launch the new apostolic wineskin.

Even though denominations have become old wineskins, when we look at their big picture we can't help but hold them in high esteem.

The New Wineskin

The new wineskin is the Spirit-filled, Spirit-led, Spirit-kept, Spirit-baptized, Spirit-gifted, saint who claims God's **grace [favor]** by accepting the **free gift** of eternal life. In the absence of grace for many years in the churches; much speculation has been accepted as truth; which in reality is a smoke screen, Satan uses to run interference with his "does God" questions:

- Does God drag people into heaven kicking and screaming against their will?

Jesus said, *"No one can come to Me unless the Father who sent Me draws him [or her]"* (John 6:44). So man's sinful nature must be changed.

- Isn't the problem with us simply that we cannot make a right decision for Christ?

No! The problem is that we possess a sinful nature that is opposed to God. We reject Christ of our own free will. If we **do** accept Christ, it will be because—*God changed our nature* so our *will* would respond *naturally* and *freely* to God's **grace [favor].** We cannot separate a person's *will* from his or her *nature.* It is the nature of a dog to bark; a cat to meow, and a human being to sin. The difference in the three is not that with humans we were **not created** to glorify and enjoy God—but that **we refuse** to accept that as the goal of our creation and existence. Different from the dog and cat whose behavior is natural—our sinful behavior is *unnatural,* rebellion of our nature.

If the unbeliever's reaction to Christ is rejection, he or she is only reacting to his or her sinful nature. If an individual has accepted Christ—the person's nature has been changed. In each case the individual makes the choice. Those not choosing Christ will be condemned and those who chose Christ will live. But we must remember—*only a move of God's **grace** can change your nature so you will say yes to Him.* (see Hebrews 11:6; Ephesians 2:8). Salvation is of the Lord (see Jonah 2:9).

Salvation is of the Lord

Many sermons have been preached with the title, "My part in salvation." The message conveyed here suggests that we contribute to our own salvation. God said it is a gift. So why do we insist on doing something to get it? Any *reference* to "our part" immediately alludes to making a salvation by **works,** not **grace;** if so salvation would be of God and humans—rather than **God alone.**

In his book, *Putting Amazing Back into Grace,* Michael Horton declares, "Not even our decision merits eternal life. If you want to talk about "our part" in salvation it's this: **sin** and **resistance."** Additionally, when we respond in faith, we are not securing our salvation; we are only reaching out for something that is already accomplished by God. [28]

John R. W. Stott speaks to this: We must never think of salvation as a kind of transaction between God and us in which He contributes **grace** and we contribute **faith.** For, we were dead and had to be **quickened** by the Spirit before we could believe. Christ's apostles clearly teach elsewhere that saving faith too is God's gracious gift."[29]

And now that Christ has come and died and thereby satisfied the Father's demands on sin, all we need to do is claim His **grace** by accepting the free gift of eternal life. Period![30]
—Charles R. Swindoll

Dr. Swindoll points out four practical expectations you can anticipate as you get a firm grasp on grace:

- *First, you can expect to gain a greater appreciation for God's gifts to you and others.*
- *Second, you can expect to spend less time and energy critical of and concerned about others' choices.*
- *Third, you can expect to become more tolerant and less judgmental.*
- *Fourth, you can expect to take a giant step toward maturity.*[31]

And so it is with our Lord. When we do things we should not, He may chasten us, sometimes quite severely, but He never turns His back nor will He send His child to hell! We do not fall from grace and need to be saved a second time. He deals with His own in grace [unmerited favor].

Certainly there will be those who as stated earlier try to live by a combination of law and grace. Like the Pharisees toward the woman taken in adultery—who pushes for us to be stern and cold. There is always that faction of old unanointed wineskins who prefer stoning to forgiving, judgment to tolerance. But there is hope that the anointed wineskins will join the ever increasing numbers of the Spirit-filled wineskins who received the Spirit's message to the churches. "Christlike grace is back! Praise the Lord!"

STUDY GUIDE: CHAPTER 7

1. Many biblical _____ were _____ as
    counterfeit _____ came into the church. PG. 57

2. Jesus died a _____ _____ for
    the _____ of the whole world PG. 58

3. Right living in the Bible is founded on two principles found in
    the Great Commandment: PG. 58

    1. _____
    2. _____

4. Jesus gave His disciples the Great Commission which actually
    are _____ _____. PG. 59

5. God affects change through the use of _____
    _____. PG 61

6. Isaiah prophesied concerning the coming of the
    _____ of God's Word. PG. 61

7. Denominations were used by God to spread
    _____ _____ around the world. PG. 63

CHAPTER 8

A Restored Concept of Ministry

"Your will be done on earth as it is in heaven" (Matthew 6:10).

We have entered a period in this country when it is evident that unless we repent and return to God's will our nation will fail. There is a saying, because a thing has been practiced for 2000 years doesn't make it right, likewise, because a thing hasn't been practiced for 2000 years doesn't make it wrong. I think that statement pretty much sums up the parody that most recognize as the American Church today.

Those of us who were trained in the old wineskins of denominations realized that only what was done in the local churches was considered authentic ministry, and what was done outside in the name of ministry was to some an abomination in the eyes of the church. The accepted presupposition was that God called *certain persons* to serve the church as pastors and other ministers. Having said that, we still believe all Christians are *called* to serve the cause of Christ in the church and the marketplace.

In spite of societal thought about separation of church and state—it all belongs to the Lord. *The earth is the Lord's, and all its fullness. The world and those that dwell therein* Psalm 24:1). That's the way the old wineskins believed and expressed it and it worked for their church concept of ministry. Today church leaders must move into the kingdom concept. In *"Anointed for Business,"* Ed Silvoso identifies four **erroneous** beliefs that have **negatively affected** believers in the workplace:

1. That there is a God-ordained division between clergy and laity.
2. That the church is called to operate primarily inside a building often referred to as a temple.
3. That people involved in business cannot be as spiritual as those serving in traditional church ministry.
4. That the primary role of marketplace Christians is to make money to support the vision of those "in the ministry."[32]

Realizing the true damage and hindrances of these four beliefs should cause those in church leadership to examine their concepts and methods of ministry. Not for one moment should we allow Society's demand for separation to sway us to forfeit the Christ-given mission [*to all creation*]. We must have a teachable spirit and make necessary changes and adjustments to bring the churches' ministries into alignment with the truths of God's Word that the Spirit is *revealing* today.

Mandatory Mind Change

As part of the new wineskin, I constantly warn pastors and other leaders that the Spirit is urgently speaking to the churches to initiate a paradigm shift from being church—centered to kingdom—centered. At issue with this shift is how we *think about* what I refer to as *present truth [that specific truth that the Spirit is speaking to the churches today].* The old wineskins' acceptance of science and reason **[the worship of man's wisdom]** as their source of revelation, coupled with reluctance to change, power struggles, theological errors due to spiritual ignorance and fear caused many truths of God's Word to be lost, misinterpreted, or ignored for convenience sake between the third and the twentieth centuries. For various reasons, the Reformation did not continue long enough for all lost biblical truth to be restored to the churches. Further confusing the issue is the ever-widening intergenerational gap between the older generation and the younger generations. It is the norm today to see four-generational families together due to longevity.

Many churches remain loyal to the Reformation form of church; but without the accompanying commitment and revelation of truth the early reformers possessed for change. As the old anointed wineskins die out in the denominations church polity turns to church politics and there goes the power of God! Many churches are replacing those dear departed saints with people like those Old Covenant believers that Paul came upon who believed in Jesus, but had not been able to fully connect the dots between John the Baptist's baptism unto repentance and that of receiving the fullness of Christ. Paul referred to these as disciples which mean "learners" or "followers" (see Acts 19:1-7).

There are many such people in the local churches today who believe on Jesus, but have not grasped the Christian faith and Christ in His fullness; which includes the manifestation in ministry of the indwelling Spirit (v. 2; Acts 1:8). The people whom Paul met believed his presentation of the *gospel* and came through *grace* to saving faith in the Lord Jesus Christ and were baptized. Although baptism is required of all Christians, it does not save you (study also Ephesians 4:5; Romans 6) for a spiritual understanding of the full significance of baptism. In Acts 2:37-38 the Scripture says,

"Now when they heard this, they were cut to their hearts, and said to Peter and the rest of the apostles, **"Men and brethren, what shall we do?"** *Then Peter said to them, "Repent, and let every one of you be baptized in the name of Jesus Christ for the remission of sins; and you shall receive the gift of the Holy Spirit.*

Then in verse 39, *"the promise . . . . All who are afar off"* [notice the promise of Acts 1:4-5: And being assembled together with them, He commanded them not to depart from Jerusalem, but to wait for the **Promise of the Father,** which, "He said, "you have heard from Me; for John truly baptized with water, but you shall be baptized with the Holy Spirit not many days from now"]. In His grace:

- God included the Gentiles also to share in the blessings of salvation (see Ephesians 2:11-13).
- As many as the Lord our God will call; as salvation is ultimately of the Lord. *"Being justified freely* **by His grace through the redemption that is in Christ Jesus** (Romans 3:24).
- Justification is a gracious gift God extends to the repentant, believing sinner, wholly separate from human merit or work.
- The believer has **access to God through Jesus Christ** (Romans 5:1).

Grace is the most crucial part of the gospel message: salvation is a **gift from God** wholly [unmerited favor] separate from any human effort or achievement (see Romans 3:24, 27; 4:1-5; 5:20, 21). For by **grace** you have been saved through **faith** and that not of yourselves; it is the gift of God, not of works, lest anyone should boast (Ephesians 2:8-9).

The presentation of the gospel [of Christ] today remains God's strategy for soul-winning notice Acts 2:41 results:

"Then those who gladly received his word were baptized; and that day about three thousand souls were added to them."

Unless the local churches leave the church-centered works-driven concept of ministry and *return* to the kingdom concept, the finished work of Christ [grace] (see Acts 1:3), they will continue to be powerless in the face of Satan's onslaught. Today many of such churches create religious forms, non-biblical programs and activities to fill the void left [without the Spirit]. The younger generations avoid or leave such churches today. The **reality** that these young people are seeking can only be produced by the **Spirit of Truth.**

The Spirit of Truth

The Holy Spirit is the Spirit of Truth. In John 14:16, Jesus promised that the Father would give the true believer another [*same kind as Himself*] Helper [*"one called alongside to help"*] that He may abide [*has to do with permanent residence in the* believer] with you forever. The Spirit of Truth would come, indwell and help the believer forever (study Romans 8:9; 1Corinthians 6:19, 20; 12:13). The Holy Spirit's coming seems to be dual (purposed):

- And when He is come He will convict [convince] the world of *sin*—because they did not believe in Jesus as Messiah and the Son of God. Notice sin is singular [the sin is rejection of the finished work of Jesus Christ] (see John 16:8).
- When He, the Spirit of Truth has come, He will *guide you into all truth . . . . He will tell you things to come . . . . He will glorify Me . . . . He will take of Mine and declare it unto you.* The purpose of the Holy Spirit's coming is not condemnation—but conviction [*to convince*] of the need for the Savior (see v. 13).

The Holy Spirit lays out Jesus' plans for His disciples:

- Love is to serve as the distinguishing characteristic of discipleship (see John 13:35). This love is produced through the New Covenant by the transforming power of the Holy Spirit (see Jeremiah 31:29-34; Ezekiel 36:24-26; Galatians 5:22).
- He is the Spirit of Truth in that He is the source of truth; and He communicates the truth to His own by indwelling and teaching them to witness and proclaim the gospel (see v. 26; 16:12-5).
- Apart from Him, humankind cannot know God's truth (see 1 Corinthians 2:12-16; 1 John 2:20, 27).
- True believers obey the Lord's commands by submitting to His Spirit and His Word.

The Holy Spirit's indwelling of believers indicates a distinction between the ministry of the Holy Spirit before and after Pentecost. While clearly the Holy Spirit has been with all who ever believed throughout redemptive history as the source of truth, faith, and life, Jesus is saying something new is coming in His ministry. John 7:37-39 indicates this *unique* ministry would be like "rivers of living water."

I bring to your attention once more the Old Covenant believers that Paul ran into who had not received the Holy Spirit in the unique fullness and intimacy (see Acts 19:-7; 1:8; 2:1-4; 1 Corinthians 12:11-13).

Satan uses secular-based religious Christianity to keep true Christians from being able to demonstrate the power and display the gospel of grace Christ commanded; that way he can limit the impact a truly transformed life should have on the world.

Without the Spirit's operation in these churches there can be no viable life or demonstration of supernatural power. Such churches have a form of godliness [works-based salvation] but deny the power [the Holy Spirit]. This was never the Lord's will for His church. Notice in John 14:15-31, Jesus promises His church (believers) supernatural blessings the kingdom of this world does not and cannot enjoy:

- A supernatural Helper (vv. 15-17).
- A supernatural life (vv. 18-19).

- A supernatural union (vv. 20-25).
- A supernatural Teacher (v. 26).
- A supernatural peace (vv. 27-31).

These supernatural blessings are for all believers. They are embedded in our love for Jesus Christ as evidenced by our love for Him and others as we stand in obedience to His commands.

Love and obedience are inseparable and are manifested in us in *fruit* produced by God in the transforming, regenerating power of the Holy Spirit. God has implanted within our hearts overflowing evidence that we belong to Him in that we love the One who first loved us (see Romans 5:5).

This love is manifested through His glorious Presence in each true believer. Sandwiched between chapters 12 and 14 of I Corinthians is chapter 13 called the love chapter; where we are told, "the greatest of these is love." Chapter 12 lists the gifts of the Spirit and chapter 14 records the operation of the gifts; however to get from Chapter 12 and the gift listings to how the gifts operate in the body of Christ requires you to go through chapter 13, love! The gifts of the Spirit can operate properly only through the love of God shed abroad in our hearts in the new birth, our God-like love.

Characteristics of that Love

1. **It suffers long**—is patient (see 1 Thessalonians 5:14).
2. **It is kind**—gentle especially with those who hurt (see Ephesians 4:32).
3. **It does not envy**—is not jealous of what others have (see Proverbs 23:17).
4. **It does not parade itself**—put itself on display (see John 3:30).
5. **It is not puffed up**—arrogance, or proud (Galatians 6:3).
6. **It does not act rudely**—Mean-spiritedly, insulting others (see Ecclesiastes 5:2).
7. **It does not seek its own**—way, or act pushy (1 Corinthians 10:24).
8. **It is not provoked**—or angered (see Proverbs 19:11).

9. **It thinks no evil**—does not keep score on others (see Hebrews 10:17).
10. **It rejoices not in iniquity**—takes no pleasure when others fall into sin (see Mark 3:5).
11. **It rejoices in the truth**—is joyful when righteousness prevails (see 2 John 4).
12. **It bears all things**—handles the burdensome (see Galatians 6:2).
13. **It believes all things**—trusts in God no matter what (see Proverbs 3:5).
14. **It hopes all things**—keeps looking up, does not despair (see Philippians 3:13).
15. **It endures all things**—puts up with everything; does not wear out (see Galatians 6:9).
16. **It never fails**—the only thing it cannot do is fail (see 1 Corinthians 16:14).[33]

The objects of faith and hope will be fulfilled and perfectly manifested in heaven, but love the God-like virtue, is everlasting (see 1 John 4:8). Heaven will be the place for the expression of nothing but perfect love toward God and each other. The implication is that such children will be recognizable by their God-like qualities.

The Sons of God

But as many as received Him, to them gave He power to become the sons of God, even to them that believe on His name: Which were born, not of blood, nor of the will of the flesh, nor of the will of man, but of God (John 1:12, 13).

In Romans 8:14, the apostle Paul expounds on an identifiable trait of the sons of God: *For as many as are **led by the Spirit of God,** they are the sons of God.* Most believers do not have a clear understanding of what this involves. When most members of local churches think of being led by the Spirit, they more than likely will picture in their minds a particular fellow Christian who makes reference to the fact that God told them to do something, and they felt compelled to obey. Certainly hearing the voice of God and acting on it is part of what it means to be led of the Spirit of God. Being led of God's Spirit (His nature) implies not only being obedient to the voice of God—but also the Holy Spirit forming the character of God within us.

God's desire that the individual characters of His children undergo a transformational process and become identical with the character of Jesus, the apostle Paul plainly states,

For whom He did foreknow, He also did predestinate to be conformed to the image of His Son, that He might be the firstborn among many brethren (Romans 8:29).

Being conformed to the image of Jesus simply means taking on His form; His likeness, and His resemblance. When all of God's children are conformed to the character and the likeness of His only begotten Son, Jesus—then and only then will it become evident that they are led by the Spirit of God; therefore truly they are the sons of God.

Developing the character of Jesus is accomplished by developing the same *fruits* that were recognized in His life. In Matthew 7, Jesus Himself taught that it is through outward manifestation [fruits] that inward nature [character] is recognized:

Beware of false prophets, which come to you in sheep's clothing, but inwardly they are ravening wolves. You will know them by their fruits. Do men gather grapes from thorn bushes or figs from thistles?

Therefore by their fruits you will know them (Matthew 7:15, 16, 20).

When Jesus said, **. . . you will know them . . . ,** He was speaking to His disciples about false prophets. The world must be able to recognize the true sons of God. **They recognize them by their fruits!** Contrary to the thinking today in many churches on this issue, Jesus did **not** say,

- You will know them by their miracles.
- You will know them by the number of members.

- You will know them by the number of meals they serve to the homeless.
- You will know them by how loudly they speak in tongues.
- You will know them by their show choirs, dancers and star-powered pastors.

Jesus said, *"Ye shall know them by their fruits."* In essence, He said, "You shall recognize My disciples by their **character.**" The character-building fruit Jesus is speaking of are listed in (Galatians 5:22, 23):

"But the fruit of the Spirit is love, joy, peace, longsuffering, kindness, goodness, faithfulness, gentleness, self-control. Against such there is no law. And those who are Christ's have crucified the flesh with its passions and desires. If we live in the Spirit, let us also walk in the Spirit."

Fruit of the Spirit

God's grace through our faith in Christ produces through fruit of the Spirit, nine character-building attitudes or characteristics that are inextricably linked with each other and are commanded of all believers:

1. Love—The Greek term is "agape" meaning the love of choice, referring not to emotional affections, physical attractions, or familial bonds, but to respect devotion, and affection that leads to willing, self-sufficient service (see John 15:13; Romans 5:8; John 3:16, 17).
2. Joy—is happiness based on unchanging divine promises and kingdom realities. It is the sense of well-being experienced by one who knows all is well in spite of favorable or non-favorable life circumstances (see John 16:20-22).
3. Peace—is the inner calm that results from confidence in one's saving relationship with Christ. Like joy, peace is not related to one's circumstances of life (see John 14:27; Romans 8:28; Philippians 4:6-7, 9).

4. Longsuffering—refers to the ability to endure injuries inflicted by others and the willingness to accept irritating or painful people and situations (see Ephesians 4:2; Colossians 3:12; 1 Timothy 1:15-16).

5. Kindness—is tender concern for others, reflected in a desire to treat others gently, just as the Lord treats all true Christians (see Matthew 11:28-29; 19:13-14; 2 Timothy 2:24).

6. Goodness—is moral and spiritual excellence manifested in active kindness (see Romans 5:7; 6:10; 2 Thessalonians 1:11).

7. Faithfulness—is loyalty and trustworthiness (see Lamentations 3:22; Philippians 2:7-9; 1 Thessalonians 5:24; Revelation 2:10).

8. Gentleness—also translated "meekness" is a humble and gentle attitude that is patiently submissive in every offense, while having no desire for revenge or retribution (see Galatians 5:23; Colossians 3:12; James 1:21).

9. Self-control—is the restraining of passions and appetites (see 1 Corinthians 9:25; 2 Peter 1:5-6).

Because of the easy accessibility of the gifts of the Spirit, there exists a tendency of many local churches to emphasize the gifts at the expense of the fruit! This is seen very readily in many of the younger churches and ministries. This poses a very dangerous threat to the next generation's churches. One of the reasons many believers prefer substitution of the gifts and good works for the fruit of God's Spirit and grace is the fruit must be cultivated and cared for requiring much time, effort and discipline. While some fruit may seem easier to develop then others, we must remember we are commanded to develop all of the fruit. None are optional!

The Generation Gap

Those churches that are hearing what the Spirit is saying to them today, are receiving much present truth as it is revealed by the Holy Spirit. If we are to move into the new wineskin our minds must be renewed. Certainly Satan is not going to just stand around watching, in fact his diabolical activities are portraying him [as an angel of light] all over the local churches' landscapes. He often appears as a [natural/fleshly thought] in the preacher, teacher or other influential individual, thus promoting his humanistic agenda which denies truth and hinders the working of God's grace. Dr. Francis Schaeffer often spoke of *truth* and what he called *true truth.*

Satan and his demons will use truth, but only to their advantage. For example there are truths; which can be expressed to define two separate scenarios within its definitions. Satan guides those who will follow him to the definition that comes natural. Although it is true in meaning it does not go far enough to define the true truth that best applies to the situation or circumstance resulting in a dual [answers] track possibilities. Many churches today follow a programmed agenda [doctrinal interpretation] established under *law* and *grace* during the Reformation in the old wineskins of denominations. This resulted in the establishing of works-salvation for some individuals and churches, and the elimination of grace [true truth]. Notice the example of the dual tracks below:

"And when He [Holy Spirit] is come He will convict the world of sin . . . ." (John 16:8). Another word for "convict" of sin is "convince" of sin. The sin is rejection of the finished work of Jesus Christ, the Son of God.

<u>**Law—Salvation [Natural Thought]**</u>	<u>**Grace—Salvation [Spiritual Thought]**</u>
Convict the world of sin results in condemnation and death. Walking after the flesh.	Christ took our sins in His body on the cross and there died for us. Therefore, there is no condemnation and no death for the believer; who is walking after the Spirit.
So he or she Strives to attain salvation through works.	*so he or she* Receives the free gift of salvation by grace through faith.

A spirit of lawlessness, permissiveness, rebellion, inclusiveness, and selfishness defines the times in which we now live. I believe the blame falls right at the feet of God's people [lack of righteousness and glory to God]. It seems that we are striving to preach the truth of God's word, but in life many follow the kingdom of this world's humanistic, materialistic, hedonistic philosophies and lifestyles. People even in some churches have begun to feel liberated and promote their sins openly simply because politicians and judges seeking their votes have passed laws that defy the moral laws of God.

The humanistic philosophies of life have spread to every foundational institution in this nation. As a result things that crept in very subtly became embedded in our daily lives. Those who are not studying the word of God and therefore do not know the truths of God's Word are vulnerable and will be more prone to believe these lies.

Only with a **"renewed mind"** will the saints of God be able to counter this invasion of subtle evil communication. Paul writes in Romans 12, verse 2:

*And do not be **conformed** to this world, but be **transformed** by the **renewing** of your mind, that you may prove what is that good and acceptable and perfect will of God.*

The New Living Translation amplifies,

*Don't copy the behavior and customs of **this world,** but let God transform you into a new person by changing the way you think . . . .*

I have emphasized three key words in the text above [conformed, transformed, and renewed] which capsules what it is to acquire a renewed mind.

- Do not be **conformed** to this world—In other words, he is saying, "Don't allow yourself to be conformed to the world. J.B. Phillips translation of this phrase reads, "Don't let the world around you squeeze you into its own mold."

Remember, Paul is talking to Christians. That means it is possible for the believer to be molded [in thinking] by the world, *instead of the Word.* "World" here can be translated "age" or "contemporary generation." Our world is secular in [thinking].

- But [instead] be **transformed**—In the Greek, this word is "metamorphe," which means, "to change from one form to another." Paul is saying, "Don't do that . . . but do this!" "Don't think that way . . . . Think this way!" "Don't go on being conformed to this world, but go on being transformed daily. A great example of transformation happens when a lowly worm spins itself into a cocoon; and after a period of time the cocoon breaks open and out flies a beautiful monarch butterfly. The worm that went in—comes out transformed something else, a butterfly.

- By the **renewing** of your mind—Paul writes that the believer is transformed by the *development of a new way of thinking*—the renewing of our minds. Renewing the mind is like deleting old files from a computer—completely erasing their presence and in their place, loading a new file that comes from the Scriptures, through which the Holy Spirit reprograms or refashions our minds. Literally, he is saying, "Allow the truth of God's Word to take up residency inside you, opening your mind to its wisdom.

- Our part is to become disciples [students or learners] of the Word. Then God uses the Word to transform our minds [thinking]. You cannot be transformed unless you are informed.

Paul's letter to these believers tells us that transformation takes place as our minds are active in the Word of God. Our minds are **then** renewed by the Word and the Spirit of God. Paul told Timothy, "Listen Timothy, I want you to be," . . . . *constantly nourished on the words of the faith and the sound doctrine which you have been following.* (1 Timothy 4:6).

95

In the following verse he wrote,

. . . . discipline [train] yourself for the purpose of godliness (1 Timothy 4:7).

We live in a generation that supposedly tolerates everything, believes nothing, and cares about no one anywhere nearly as much as themselves. The kingdom of this world led by the prince of this world, Satan has revved up his philosophy of Secular humanism. Secular humanism is a way of thinking that says, "be as healthy as you can; live as long as you can; get as rich as you can; be as comfortable as you can." This mindset defines the world's thinking whereby man is the measure of all things. We will fully engage this topic in the next chapter.

Recent Barna research reflects that just over three-quarters or (77%) of Americans "believe the values and morals of America are declining." And when asked what is to blame for the "decline:"

- One-third of Americans (32%) attributes that shift to a lack of Bible reading. This is a greater percentage of people than point to:
- The "negative influence of media" (29%) or:
- "Corruption from corporate greed" (25%).
- Similarly, nearly six out of ten (56%) believe the Bible has too little influence in American society—that's more than four times the percentage of people who think the Bible has too much influence (13%).

Millions of Americans believe our society needs the Bible; and believe the Bible's moral teachings will help the next generation:

- Nearly half (46%) of adults believe the Bible doesn't have much impact on American youth.

Perhaps that explains why two-thirds (66%) think public schools should teach values found in the Bible. What is the main reason for holding that viewpoint?

- Three-quarters (75%) of those supporting this believe "the Bible teaches moral principles that are badly needed in society."
- Still, even among those who contend public schools should teach about the Bible, almost half (45%) say they **would be** concerned about "favoring one religion over another."
- One-quarter of adults who support teaching about the Bible in public education (25%) say there is no legitimate reason not to teach the Bible in public schools.[34]

Despite the perception that Scripture hasn't impacted the nation's youth:

- Mosaics (ages 18-28) actually tend to show more interest in what the Bible has to say on certain issues than do older adults.
- Four out of ten Mosaics (40%) say they are interested in the Bible's wisdom on dealing with illness and death, compared with about one-quarter of all adults (28%) who say the same.
- More than one-third of Mosaics (35%) are interested in the Bible's perspective on dating and relationships.
- And four out of ten (42%) of Mosaics want to know what the Scriptures say about parenting—both of those percentages are much higher than the norms.[35]

Millions of Americans say the Bible can help them address life's twists, turns and troubles. This is particularly true of Mosaics (ages 18-28) who Barna reports are more likely than average to show interest in the Bible's wisdom on the topics below:[36]

Interested in the Bible's wisdom on:	All adults	Mosaics
Dealing with illness/ death	28%	33%
Addressing family conflict	24%	40%

Parenting	22%	42%
Romance and sexuality	17%	30%
Dating and relationships	16%	35%
The influence of technology	12%	14%
Dealing with divorce	8%	14%

Barna goes on to report that despite a clear cultural interest and awareness of the Bible, the research also shows that neutral or negative attitudes toward the Bible are becoming more commonplace.

- In 2011, more than half (53%) of adults said the Bible "contains everything a person needs to live a meaningful life.
- In 2013, that percentage dipped below half of the population (47%).
- Although the 61% of American adults who want to read the Bible represents a majority of Americans, it's a step down from the 67% of adults who said the same in 2011.
- Furthermore, the percentage of adults who believe the Bible contains everything a person needs to live a meaningful life has declined substantially from 75% to 66% in the last two years.[37]

Conflicting Communications

In "One Church Four Generations" Gary l. McIntosh suggests there are four generations, existing together, and therefore, four sets of value systems that are being advanced, each with its perceived needs and perspectives.

Church leaders must understand:

- Each generation's values.
- How their values, were molded by events that define that particular generation.

He defines a generation—a group of people who are connected by their place in time with common boundaries and a common character. We can say that those people are of a certain generation:

- Their ages may vary widely.
- They tend to identify with each other because of national or world events they have all experienced.[9/11 for example].
- Fads they have enjoyed.
- Prominent people they have come to know.
- They tend to share certain character traits or characteristics that reflect their time in history.
- They are loosely held together by these experiential threads and by some common beliefs.
- They do some things in ways unique to the group, and tend to see differences between themselves and members of other groups.

According to McIntosh we can fit most people into four broad groups:

- Late sixties and above are called—Builders also called [Seniors].
- Forties to mid-sixties—Boomers.
- Late twenties to late thirties—Busters.
- Eighteen to twenty nine—Bridgers also called [Mosaics or Millennia].

As a generation moves through time, it causes a generational wave or change. Many members of a group will move through childhood, young adult, midlife, and retirement as a group, although the youngest and oldest members of the group will experience these phases at different times.[38]

The sins that are causing this downward spiral of morality in the culture are being redefined or simply put on the list of unmentionables. Many people even some Christians who are in position and can effect change think that politicians can supply the necessary legislation to fix the problems [these people are willing to try anything—that is as long as it **excludes** God and the things of

God!]. The answers or solutions to America's problems can only be found in God's Word. When things made by man break down we will go to any extreme to find the answer including going back to the manufacturer; but God who made the world and all that is in it is not to be considered in man's problem solving process. Hear the Word of the Lord,

"The wicked shall be turned into hell, and all nations that forget God" (Psalm 9:17).

Illegitimacy is now celebrated, along with abortions. Our secularized education system has imbedded the humanistic ideal that there are no absolutes, no moral boundaries, and no dogma. Truth is reduced to your opinion. And don't try to cram your opinion down someone else's throat. Many Christians and local churches in America have allowed the secular culture to squeeze them into these mind sets. Such thinking is the norm for the kingdom of this world—but not the kingdom of God. To true Christianity this thinking violates the Word of God (see Romans 12:2).

To the Secular humanists, human beings are **animals**; and that explains how a judge can give a man a sentence of thirty days in jail for raping a teenage girl; or an educator can sexually abuse children as long as no one is hurt, they quip. Unless the churches decide that enough is enough and exposes this amoral humanistic mindset; with its gross sins it will continue and grow worse. Have you wondered why Christianity is becoming less and less influential? There was a day when men and women sought higher offices to insure the Christian consensus was represented. Today that consensus is not there because we've obeyed the humanists and secular culture and left such things to them. That's why I believe the Holy Spirit is pulling anointed old wineskins out as He did in the case of John the Baptist, Martin Luther and many others through the centuries to launch the new wine of "recovered grace."

I believe this is the most radical shift ever; as the belief systems of many prominent old wineskins are being shaken to the core. In fact, there is an on going exodus from the pulpit of non-anointed ministers, who refuse to hear what the Spirit is saying to the churches; and yet there is a much larger number of them who remain in leadership being used of the devil and his kingdom [knowingly or unknowingly of the collateral damage they are inflicting upon the body of Christ] as they hinder God's new wineskin.

Longevity seems to be their yardstick and they hang on even though the pews are emptying at an alarming rate. They claim to have tried every thing in the old wineskin's denomination rule book, but to no avail. I stated in an earlier section that many today as with the Galatians moved into a flawed theology which teaches that *I am saved by* **grace** *through* **faith** *but perfected through* **the flesh** (human effort). The legalistic establishment is fiercely resisting, but this Spirit anointed movement is being embraced with joy and great enthusiasm by many who are deeply dissatisfied, spiritually tormented, and tired of playing church.

Those who are listening to the Spirit are waking up to the revelation and restoration of God's great gospel of grace. Notice what Paul says in II Corinthians 4:15:

"For all things are for your sakes, so that the **grace** *which is spreading to more and more people may cause the giving of thanks abound to the glory of God."*

Praise God, the Spirit of Truth is moving among us, and He is revealing what has been hidden under centuries of religious double-talk. **Grace** is spreading to more and more people as the new wineskin grows causing the giving of thanks to abound to the glory of God.

The Perfect Will of God

We have a new move of thought as we experience a great restoration of the truths of God's Word concerning the grace of our heavenly Father in the finished work of His dear Son. One of the characteristics of the seeking bridgers [young people] is reality. The great awakening of grace will change our understanding of God and the will of God in ways beyond our expectations. **Grace without the mixing with law** is the starting restored truth for this on-going great restorative move of God. In his book, "Living on the Raged Edge," Dr. Charles Swindoll tells the story of a fourth century monk who spent most of his life in a remote community of prayer, studying and raising his vegetables for the cloister's kitchen. When he was not tending his garden spot, he was happily fulfilling his vocation of study and prayer.

Then one day this monk, whose name was Telemachus felt the Lord was leading him to go to Rome, the political center of the world—the busiest, wealthiest, biggest city in the world. Telemachus wondered why he was being drawn to Rome. He didn't fit Rome. He fit this little, quite place, the cloistered community, this sheltered little garden where his convictions were deepening and his faith in God was strong. But he couldn't fight God's direction. So he left.

By and by, he found his way to the busy streets of Rome, and he was stunned by what he saw. The people were preoccupied. They were angry. They were violent, in fact. And on one occasion the bewildered little monk was swept up in the group, pushed along by the crowd. Finally he wound up in a place he didn't even know existed—the coliseum—where animalistic gladiators fought and killed one another for little reason other than the amusement of the thousands that gathered in Rome's public stadium.

He stared in disbelief as one gladiator after another stood before the emperor and said, "We who are about to die salute thee." He put his hands to his ears when he heard the clashing of swords and shields, as one man after another fought to his death.

He could stand it no longer. But what in the world could he do? He was nothing! Still, he ran and jumped up on top of the perimeter wall and cried, "In the name of Christ, forbear!" He could not bear the senseless killing. "Stop this now!"

No one listened. They kept applauding the fight as it went on. Another man fell. Finally, unable to contain himself, he jumped down onto the sandy floor of the arena. What a comic figure he must have appeared to be—of slight build, a small man in a monk's habit, dashing back and forth between muscular, brutal fighters. Again, he shouted, "In the name of Christ, forbear!"

The crowd looked at him and sneered, and one of the gladiators, with his shield, bumped him aside and went after his opponent. Finally, he became an irritation to the crowd as well as the gladiators. Someone in the stands yelled, "Run him through! Kill him!"

The same gladiator that had pushed him aside with his shield came down against his chest and opened his stomach with one flash of the sword. As he slumped to his knees, the little monk gasped once more, "In the name of Christ . . . forbear!"

Then a strange thing occurred. As the two gladiators and the crowd focused on the sill form on the suddenly crimson sand, the arena grew quiet. In the silence, someone in the top tier got up and walked out. Another followed. All over the arena, spectators began to leave, until the huge stadium was emptied.

There were other forces at work, of course, but that innocent figure lying in the pool of blood crystallized the opposition, and that was the **last gladiatorial contest** in the Roman Coliseum. Never again did men kill each other for the crowd's entertainment in the Roman arena.[39] In Esther 4:14, Esther agreed to intervene [risking her life!] with the king on behalf of her people. The Lord challenges each of us to know our purpose and calling in Christ and get to it:

> *For if you remain completely silent at this time,*
> *relief and deliverance*
> *will arise for the Jews*
> *from another place,*
> *but you and your father's house will perish.*
> *Yet who knows*
> *whether you have come to the kingdom*
> ***for such a time as this?"***

Grace that Saves

STUDY GUIDE: CHAPTER 8

1. There is a God ordained division between clergy and laity. T or F. PG. 67

2. Define "present truth". PG. 68

3. Many in the local churches have not grasped the _____ _____ nor evidence of the indwelling _____ PG. 68

4. Local churches must leave the _____ _____ concept of ministry and return to the _____ _____ PG. 69

5. Love is the _____ _____ of discipleship. PG. 69

6. The true believers _____ the Lord's commands by _____ to His Spirit and His _____. PG. 70

7. Satan and his demons will use _____ but only to their _____. PG. 70

8. Only with a _____ _____ will the saints of God be able to _____ the invasion. PG. 70

9. McIntosh believes there are _____ _____ existing together. PG. 79

10. To the secular humanists human beings are _____. PG. 79

11. Grace without the _____ of _____ is restored truth. PG. 80

12. Mosaics (ages 18-28) are more interested in Biblical wisdom than the average person. PG. 77

SECTION III

GRACE IS SUFFIECIENT

CHAPTER 9

INTERGENERATIONAL INVOLVEMENT

A generation of young Christians are growing up and moving into church leadership feeling that they have been duped by the traditional church. Though they were raised in the traditional church they are experiencing an intergenerational gap. The community they were raised up in no longer understands their frustrations, struggles, and mind sets. To express their doubts places them in dire straights with many of the old-timers in the church. Considering the condition the world is in these young people view their seniors' suggestions suspiciously, while the seniors are observing them as incapable of taking over.

As an anointed old wineskin, I trust that God already has the leadership worked out. **His true** leaders will be alright because as in all generations they will be God-fearing, Spirit-filled saints who hear what the Spirit is saying to His churches. Dissatisfied with the old wineskins of denominations' programmed lack of reality, the younger generations are trying new forms of worship and service. They are not church-minded like the old wineskin [denominations], but are kingdom-minded.

Getting a handle on Reality

America is a complex society. Our population is probably the most diverse of any nation in the world—ethnically, religiously, socially, and economically. On the other hand, the challenges associated with population diversity have demanded a stiff price on our culture. I will list a few:

- The differing and often conflicting values and belief systems due to secular humanism and multiculturalism's contributions to a negative attitude toward God's moral law which is plaguing our nation today.
- The process of assimilating people into a progressive cultural mix is proving to be a very difficult challenge as is apparent in the fast growing disparities between young and

old, rich and poor, educated and uneducated, and married and single.

- The ever rising tensions between true Christianity and religious Christianity, conservatives and liberals, Christians and non-Christians, legitimacy and illegitimacy; the government and courts' redefinition of marriage and the family along with the differing views concerning gender orientation.
- Racial and ethnic tensions continue to trouble the nation, in spite of gains made.

For the past several years, hostility, mistrust, chaos, apathy, lack of effective leadership and productivity are some of the most pointed outcomes as these conflicts remain in an unresolved stalemate and seems to be settling into a "we/ they" attitude.

Secular Humanism

While the media tracks other world events across the globe, Secular humanism, the kingdom of this world's greatest evil and most deceptive of all philosophies whether religious or not is at work dismantling our nation's foundational institutions through reorientation and redefinition, especially knowledge, marriage and the family, education and government. It is important that every Christian know the subtle ways that Secular humanism is manifesting itself all around us and undermining the true biblical worldview. To begin:

- Humanists do not believe God exists and therefore their worldview says mankind is the highest entity [man is the measure of all things].
- Humanists believe the Bible to be the work of men [perhaps with a religious ax to grind].
- Humanists believe evolution is the only way to explain the existence of life, since he or she denies the existence of God.
- Humanists see man as basically good.
- Humanists believe that some things are right for some people and even some situations that may be wrong for other people and other situations are right for them.

- Humanists believe that there is no absolute right and wrong; and everything depends on the situation.
- Humanists' life goal is since this physical life is all there is, our goal is to get as much happiness and gain and as many things as I can before time runs out and I cease to exist.
- Humanists believe that since man is merely a highly evolved animal, some human life is not special therefore the humanists support abortion, euthanasia, and even infanticide in some cases.
- Humanists believe that since man is merely a highly evolved animal, sexual gratification is not to be denied as long as "it doesn't hurt anyone." [The humanist is often shortsighted about what kind of behavior "hurts" others].
- Humanists believe that since man is merely a highly evolved animal, no sexual acts should be considered improper as long as "it doesn't hurt anyone."
- Humanists view man as the supreme being of the universe.
- Humanists reject the existence of God and the supernatural.
- Humanists see moral values as relative and changing and varying from person to person.
- Humanists seek to eradicate biblical Christianity.[40]

The Scripture warns, *"See to it that no one takes you captive through philosophy and empty deception, according to the tradition of men, according to the elementary principles of the world, rather than according to Christ"* (Colossians 2:8 AMP).

What is Secular Humanism?

The Council for Secular humanism says, "It is a term which has come about in the last thirty years to describe a world view with the following elements and principles:

- A conviction that dogmas, ideologies and traditions, whether religious, political, or social, must be weighed and tested by each individual and not simply accepted on faith.
- A commitment to the use of critical reason, factual evidence, and scientific methods of inquiry, rather than faith and

mysticism, in seeking solutions to human problems and answers to important human questions.

- A primary concern for fulfillment, growth, and creativity for both the individual and humankind in general.
- A constant search for objective truth, with the understanding that new knowledge and experience constantly alter our imperfect perception of it.
- A concern for this life and a commitment to making it meaningful through better understanding of ourselves, our history, our intellectual and artistic achievements, and outlooks of those who differ from us.
- A search for viable individual, social and political principles of ethical conduct, judging them on their ability to enhance human well-being and individual responsibility.
- A conviction that with reason, an open marketplace of ideas, good will, and the "new," tolerance, progress can be made in building a better world for ourselves and our children.[41]

How Do Secular Humanists View Religious and Supernatural Claims?

Secular humanists accept a world view or philosophy called naturalism, in which the physical laws of the universe are not superseded by non-material or supernatural entities such as demons, gods, or other "spiritual" beings outside the realm of the natural universe. Supernatural events such as miracles (in which physical laws are defied) and psi phenomena, such as ESP, telekinesis, etc., are not dismissed as out of hand, but are viewed with a high degree of skepticism.

Are Secular Humanists Atheists?

Secular humanists are generally non-theists. They typically describe themselves as nonreligious. They hail from widely divergent philosophical and religious backgrounds.

Secular Humanism places trust in intelligence rather than divine guidance.[42]

Thus secular humanists do not rely upon gods or other supernatural forces to solve their problems or provide guidance for this conduct. They rely instead upon the application of reason, the lessons of history, and personal experience to form an ethical/moral foundation and to create meaning in life. Secular humanists look to the methodology of science as the most reliable source of information about what is factual or true about the universe we all share, acknowledging that new discoveries will always alter and expand our understanding of it and perhaps change our approach to ethical issues as well. In any case their outlook draws primarily from human experiences and scientific knowledge.[43]

What is the Origin of Secular Humanism?

Secular humanism as an organized philosophical system is relatively new, but its foundations can be found in the ideas of classical Greek philosophers such as the Stoics and Epicureans as well as in Chinese Confucianism. Those philosophical views looked to human beings rather than gods to solve human problems.

During the Middle Ages of Western Europe, humanist philosophers were suppressed by the political power of the church. Those who dared to express views in opposition to the prevailing religious dogmas were banished, tortured or executed. Not until the Renaissance of the fourteenth to seventeenth centuries, with the flourishing of art, music, literature, philosophy and exploration, would give consideration of the humanist alternative to a god-centered existence be permitted. During the Enlightenment of the eighteenth century, with the development of science, philosophers finally began to openly criticize the authority of the church and engage in what became known as "free thought."

The nineteenth century Freethinking movement of America and Western Europe finally made it possible for the common citizen to reject blind faith and superstition without the risk of persecution. The influence of science and technology, together with the challenges to religious orthodoxy by such celebrity freethinkers as Mark Twain and Robert G. Ingersoll brought elements of humanist philosophy even to mainline Christian churches, which became more concerned with this world and less with the next.

In the twentieth century scientists, philosophers, and progressive theologians began to organize in an effort to promote the humanist alternative to traditional faith-based world views. These early organizers classified humanism as a non-theistic religion which would fulfill the human need for an ordered ethical/philosophical system to guide one's life, "spirituality" without the supernatural. In the last thirty years, those who reject the supernatural as a viable philosophical outlook have adopted the term "secular humanism" to describe their non-religious life stance.

Critics often try to classify secular humanism as a religion. Yet secular humanism lacks essential characteristics of a religion, including belief in a deity and an accompanying transcendent order. Secular humanists contend that issues concerning ethics, appropriate social and legal conduct, and the methodologies of science are philosophical and are not part of the domain of religion, which deals with the supernatural, mystical, and transcendent.

Secular humanism then is a philosophy and world view which centers upon human concerns and employs rational and scientific methods to address the wide range of issues important to us all. Secular humanism is at odds with faith-based religious systems on many issues.[44]

In recent years, humanists have become so **well-placed** in our society and occupy such powerful positions at all levels of family life, education, branches of government, and the professions of the marketplace in general that they **no longer** try to **conceal** their true interests but openly acknowledge their beliefs. They are no doubt convinced that it is too late for the pro-moral people of our country to eject them from offices or positions of public trust and influence. I do not agree! I am convinced that if we with much prayer, intense study of the truths of God's Word, and Spiritual guidance expose the *teachings* and *stated objectives* of Secular humanism to enough people, we can turn back to moral sanity in this great nation. It will start with your clear understanding of what humanists really are and why they are doing it. I truly believe this is a life or death [*of a nation*] situation which America faces and Christ is our only hope!

I say again! "The wicked shall be turned into hell and **all nations** that forget God" (Psalm 9:7).

Where is the Church?

Most churches continue to pursue their same old one-size-fits-all ministry approach, while the culture in which we live is too diverse and values tailored too highly to expect us to meet every need. However, we continue to press forward implementing a single set of outdated and irrelevant programs, and events. To be effective we must start with ourselves:

- Learn to focus our efforts and look at what we have to offer to others.
- Insure that our offerings are relevant, beneficial, and accessible.
- Recognize the spirituality gap between what we preach and what we live.
- Recognize the generations' communication gap and [builders and boomers resistance to change].
- Recognize that our younger segments of the population have grown accustomed to living in our ethnically diverse society.
- Recognize the fact that our secular government has redefined gender, marriage and the family.
- Realize that color of skin no longer determines race and ethnicity.
- Recognize that humanism is **not** our friend; it has devastated every institution in this nation especially family, education, and government and they are subtly blasting the foundational truths of biblical Christianity.
- Repentance and forgiveness of racial attitudes, unfounded assumptions, and unrealistic expectations related to racial diversity. Eleven a.m. on Sundays continues to be our most segregated hour of the week; and we continue to talk about spending eternity together, yet most of our church cemeteries remain more segregated than our worship services.

- Special attention must be paid to the retention of those 18-29 years old. Unlike prior generations, they are leaving the churches and not returning upon entering marriage or careers.
- Insure that our solutions help and not hinder. What worked ten years ago does not necessarily work the same today.

God showered His grace upon this nation from its birth. The United States is a nation born out of the Christian consensus of the Reformation. The word "consensus" means agreement in opinion, testimony, or belief.[45] Historians credit the unique checks and balances as the reason for its longevity. It came from the founders' understanding that human nature was not to be trusted and that humanity functions best when subject to checks and balances. Of course all of the founding fathers were not Christians, but the Christian consensus of the day was so strong concerning the fallen nature of man, that history's greatest Constitution was designed under God around it.

When I entered the Army in the 50's the Christian consensus was alive and well. We were marched to the Chapel of our choice on Sundays for Protestant, Jewish or Catholic services. On Wednesdays we were marched to one hour of character guidance. On the wall in the Dayroom was a picture of General George Washington kneeling in prayer [in full uniform]. In our leadership manual [Technical Manual 22-100] God was among the solutions for problem solving.

However, during the 60's all of that went out the window as the cigar chopping Generals became leadership's mainstay and the psychologists became our character guider. We had draftees in those days. They were older than most of us. That was great for two reasons, one, many of them had wives and children and helped us 18 and 19'ers with a lot of wisdom and life choices. The second blessing came over the years as these draftees went back into civilian life.

I made a career of the Army and as I traveled throughout the nation [early 60's] I always had a uniform hanging in the back. Those veterans were everywhere. As an African American soldier traveling with my wife Magdalene to and from duty stations during that time especially in the south and mid-west that uniform acted as a conversation piece and "pass." Veterans were everywhere! Upon my return from Vietnam in August 1968, I had to conceal my uniform and travel in civilian clothing. What a change.

Even during the turmoil of the 60's God did not forsake His church. I noticed the Spiritual change in the churches. As a P.K. growing up during the late forties and early fifties in rural North Carolina though my father was a pastor, he was also the community minister. He engaged in counseling sessions with saints and sinners alike in our home, hospital visitations, performed marriages and numerous funerals within the community. He was available.

For the most part in those days pastors were farmers or they were bi-vocational. However, the **60's** saw more churches calling pastors into full-time ministry. The pastor joined the full-time evangelist called and clarified a decade earlier **50's** i.e. Dr. Billy Graham. I was called into a Bible-teaching ministry in the early **70's** as were thousands of others, teacher returned to the body. We can see from this that Christ began restoring His gifts [see Ephesians 4:11] to the body of Christ during this period and continues the **80's** witnessed the return of the prophet, the **90's** brought back the apostle and I believe the New Testament saints returned in **2000** and continues today. Years before the mighty move of God in the body of Christ, He restored the Holy Spirit [with the gift of "speaking in tongues"] to the body of Christ during the Azusa Street Revival of **1906** extended to 1909 initiated by a black Texas preacher named William J. Seymour in Los Angeles, California. This revival marked the return of the Spiritual gifts to the church beginning with the gift of tongues. Today the Spirit has revealed about twenty four more Spiritual gifts and the worldwide Pentecostal movement [later joined by the Charismatic Movement has carried the gifts of the Spirit across denominational lines in the saints] and continues to flourish today with the fastest growing churches worldwide.[46]

The Right-Hand of God in Christ

Jesus said, ". . . . *On this Rock I will build My church, and the gates of Hades shall not prevail against it"* (Matthew 16:18b). Several interpretations have surfaced concerning this passage:

- One says death will not vanquish the Church.
- Another, one day, by the power of Christ's resurrection, the church and all the redeemed will be resurrected.
- Others suggest that the phrase means that the forces of evil will not be able to conquer the people of God.[47]

The Christian consensus has given us bountiful grace [favor] with God as a nation. Though every person does not know or acknowledge God, most still respect His moral laws for one reason or another. There remains an army of saints who respects His moral laws. Most of the Pentecostal/ Charismatic groups can claim some lineage linking them to the Azusa Street Revival and William Seymour. Seymour not only rejected the existing racial barriers in favor of "unity in Christ", he also rejected the then almost-universal barriers to women in any form of church leadership.

It became the subject of intense investigation by more mainstream Protestants. Some left feeling that Seymour's views were heresy, while others accepted his teachings and returned to their own congregations to expound them. The resulting movement became widely known as "Pentecostalism", likening it to the manifestations of the Holy Spirit recorded as occurred in the first two chapters of the Book of Acts.[48]

In the body of Christ today, many leaders are called "pastors" who actually function in the office of apostle, prophet, teacher, or even evangelists [Prayerfully study Ephesians 4]. Some who are not actually called as a fivefold minister may be trying to serve as pastors. I say "trying" because here again we run into people who began in the Spirit, but are trying to finish the race in the flesh. These ministers to be effective must recognize the paradigm shift from the church concept of ministry to the kingdom or body concept of ministry. The kingdom concept of ministry recognizes the Holy Spirit's ministry with His activating the Spiritual gifts in the saints. Many churches continue to this day rejecting the truths of God's Word restored to the body of Christ at Azusa Street concerning the Holy Spirit and the gifts. He gives the saints gifts to empower and equip them for the work of ministry [edification and evangelism], today using the fivefold ministers.[49] Notice their equipping work in the body of Christ as the result of those whom Christ gave to the church for that work (see Ephesians 4:11). The body of Christ is built up; **the final goal is maturity, truth, love and service**:

Apostles—give building strategy and lay foundations along with the prophet, in the lives of people and the local church. Biblical examples of apostles' ministry to the saints reveal that they help found and **ground the saints in the foundations of the faith and present truth** as part of the foundation of the Church; apostles are often sent to establish new works and then support those works. As initiators and those who help provide structure and leadership— apostles make a place for the saints. They provide platforms where others can serve God through their unique gifting. Some apostles not only demonstrate the supernatural but are able to activate the saints in their power gifts of the Spirit.[50]

Prophets—help bring vision, spiritual insight, revelation, and activation of new saints' supernatural gifts and callings. They do this best through their prophesying and revelation knowledge. All fivefold ministers are to minister the Logos Word to the saints, but the prophets have a **special ability to minister a Rhema Word** that personally enlightens and activates faith in the saints. Some prophets use their gifts of discernment to bring warnings about the plans of the enemy or of potential pitfalls to be avoided.[51]

Evangelists—have a special anointing to stir up the zeal of the Lord in the saints. They have an anointing and passion for **winning the lost** and making them active members of the body of Christ. The evangelists also help keep the saints focused outwardly on the need to bring the kingdom of God to the entire world. They impart to the saints the need to take blessings we have received and use them to bless others.[52]

Pastors—truly gifted pastors have the ability **to nurture, stabilize, grow, and mature the saints.** They specialize in building character, faithfulness, and family relationship in the local church family. No matter how many prophecies you have received about a mighty ministry, you will never fully reach your destiny without maturity. This is best developed by being submitted to godly leadership, and being allowed to develop little by little, just as a child does. Even those who have reached spiritual adulthood need to remain in committed relationship with those who have been **charged to keep guard over their souls.**[53]

Teachers—help prepare the saints in the milk and meat of the truth of the Word of God. A true teacher who is an extension of Christ the Master Teacher has the special ability to teach the truth of God's Word with simplicity and revelation, enlightening and enabling the saints in the Word of God. A wise teacher brings out his or her treasure both old, foundational truths and newly restored truth. We are all to study the Bible for ourselves. And we can all offer something to bless others. James 3:1 states that teachers will receive a stricter judgment. Therefore we must know and rightly divide the Word of truth.[54]

Saints—Notice, each minister has a portion of the ministry and character of Christ to impart and activate within the saints. Every saint will fulfill his or her own membership ministry but will **manifest** more of one of the fivefold natures of Christ. This is especially true in the local churches. If the pastor is an evangelist, the saints will be more evangelistic. The kingdom of God is on the earth; but because of a lack of knowledge and spiritual immaturity many local churches are not fully aware of that truth.

The Baptism of the Spirit and Unity

Another destructive force along with Secular humanism hindering the church today is religious Christianity. Divisions and personality difference among the membership due to folks walking in the flesh instead of walking in the Spirit have destroyed lives, families, and brought the gospel of Jesus Christ to non-effect in many communities. The Scripture commands us to, *"Be filled with the Spirit"* (see Ephesians 5:18). If the local church is to fulfill its Christ directed purpose and mission—the saints must live in unity by living in the Spirit. Unity is the ultimate goal when equipping for spiritual life and service. Years ago I had to go through jungle operations training in Panama. Part of the course was cross country navigation [through the jungle]. The objective was to complete the course, intact. We were sent out in five-men teams and to pass the course we had to return as a team intact. If one was lost we had to find him, if one was wounded we had to treat the wounds and carry him by no means could we leave anybody. To accomplish this mission everyone had to carry their share of the load and share their abilities, special skills, and training for the good of all. We were one when we left, one on the mission and one when we crossed the finishing line. Unity is one! In Ephesians 4:3, Paul exhorts the church to:

*"Be eager to maintain the **unity** of the spirit in the bond of peace."*

Normally when we speak of baptism we think of submersion under water, for others it is sprinkling. Then there are those who perform infant baptism. Others say baptism must be performed only upon adults who understand the meaning of the faith and baptism. Much discussion is raised over the physical event at the expense of non-clarity of the spiritual. The Scripture says,

"For by One Spirit we were all baptized into one body; whether Jews or Greeks, whether slaves or free, and have all been made to drink into one Spirit" (1 Corinthians 12:13).

The baptism in the Spirit makes even more public our membership in the body of Christ. With the baptism of the Holy Spirit we are one! The oneness or unity of Jesus' Body—that is the ultimate purpose of the baptism of the Holy Spirit.[55]

However, in the baptism of the Holy Spirit is also a supernatural seal that is given to each individual member by which Jesus Christ acknowledges him or her as part of His body, made one with Him in His death, burial and resurrection. John the Baptist declared,

". . . . This is the One that baptizes with the Holy Spirit" (John 1:33).

The unity of the Spirit baptism will be produced in the individual by the Spirit. Apart from this unity, any other method of striving to achieve any unity is impossible—many local churches settle for just being united. Just remember united is not one, but many together and therefore are not unity!

Love and Unity

In John 17, Jesus said that our love and unity would be a witness to the world. He prayed that Christians *"may all be one . . . . that the world may believe that thou hast sent Me"* (v. 21 KJV). The degree to which we allow division and hostility to reign in the church is the degree to which the flesh is allowed to block the Spirit's work in and through us and the church (study Romans 8:1-8; 7:15-20). Our witness can be neutralized by an unwillingness to maintain the unity which the Spirit has already produced in us. The world pays little attention to a divided church.

It is important also that we meet together (see Hebrews 10:25) for worship, fellowship [koinonia] and to carryout our love [agape] in "one another" ministry. The New Testament puts great emphasis on the need for Christians to know one another closely and intimately enough to be able to bear one another's burdens, confess faults to one another, encourage, exhort, and admonish one another; and minister to one another with Word, song, and prayer [true unity].

The younger generation [who loves to see action on the Word] is interested in the "one another" ministries. There are over fifty *"one another statements"* and *"commands"* in the New Testament which call us to a special kind of life together—what we call in this book:

"GRACE THAT SAVES"

The following statements and commands are in the NIV:

- "Be at peace with one another" (Mark 9:50).
- "Wash one another's feet" (John 13:14).
- "Love one another" (John 18:34).
- "Love one another" (John 13:35).
- "Love one another" (John 15:12).
- "Love one another" (John 15:17).

- "Be devoted to one another in brotherly love" (Romans 12:10).
- "Honor one another above yourselves" (Romans 12:10).
- "Love in harmony with one another" (Romans 12:16).
- "Love one another" (Romans 13:8).
- "Stop passing judgment on one another" (Romans 14:13).
- "Accept one another, then, just as Christ accepted you" (Romans 15:7).
- "Instruct one another" (Romans 15:14).
- "Greet one another with a holy kiss" (Romans 16:16).
- "When you come together to eat, wait for one another" (1 Corinthians 11:33).
- "Have equal concern for one another" (1 Corinthians 12:25).
- "Greet one another with a holy kiss" (1 Corinthians 16:20).
- "Greet one another with a holy kiss" (2 Corinthians 13:12).
- "Serve one another in love" (Galatians 5:18).
- "If you keep on biting and devouring one another . . . . you will be destroyed by each other" (Galatians 5:15).
- "Let us not become conceited, provoking and envying one another" (Galatians 5:26).

Barna surveys results show that those 18-29 years of age are more interested in the "one another" ministries than older generations.

- "Teach one another" (Colossians 3:16).
- "Admonish one another" (Colossians 3:16).
- "Make your love increase and overflow for one another" (1 Thessalonians 3:12).
- "Love one another" (1 Thessalonians 4:9).
- "Encourage one another" (1 Thessalonians 4:18).
- "Encourage one another" (1 Thessalonians 5:11).
- "Build one another up" (1 Thessalonians 5:11).
- "Encourage one another daily" (Hebrews 3:
- "Spur one another on toward love and good deeds" (Hebrews 10:24).
- "Encourage one another" (Hebrews 10:25).

- "Do not slander one another" (James 4:11).
- "Do not grumble against one another" (James 5:9).
- "Confess your sins to one another" (James 5:16).
- "Pray for one another" (James 5:16).
- "Love one another deeply from the heart" (1 Peter 1:22).
- "Live in harmony with one another" (1 Peter 3:8).
- "Love one another deeply" (1 Peter 4:8).
- Offer hospitality to one another without grumbling" (1 Peter 4:9).
- "Each one should use whateve3r gift he [or she] has received to serve one another" (1 Peter 4:10).
- "Clothe yourself with humility toward one another" (1 Peter 5:5).
- "Greet one another with a kiss of love" (1 Peter 5:14).
- "Love one another" (1 John 3:11).
- "Love one another" (1 John 3:23).
- "Love one another" (1 John 4:7).
- "Love one another" (1 John 4:11).
- "Love one another" (1 John 4:12).
- "Love one another" (2 John 5).

It is obvious that these "one another ministries" operating in the body of Christ are very important to God, since He speaks of them frequently in the Scriptures. This is in line with Jesus' exhortations to His disciples:

"A new commandment I give to you,
that you love one another;
even as I have loved you,
that you also love one another.
By this
all men will know
that that you are My disciples,
If you have love for one another" (John 13:35).

Unmerited Favor

I stated in an earlier section, that grace is almost too good to be true! It does seem too good to be true. But it is true! Liberty, freedom, joy, peace, spiritual passion, hope and so many other benefits are ours as we grasp the restored truth of the gospel of **grace, [unmerited favor]**. Certainly God's favor in our lives should humble us, and focus our love on Him and others. To fully grasp the gospel of grace is to live according to the Spirit in holiness and obedience under the Lordship of Christ. He is LORD!

"For those who live according to the flesh set their minds on the things of the flesh, but those who live according to the Spirit, the things of the Spirit" (Romans 8:5)

The Greek word rendered **set their minds** includes a person's will, thoughts, and emotions. It also includes assumptions, values, desires, and purposes. Setting the mind **on the things of the flesh** or on **the things of the Spirit** means being oriented to or governed by those things on which we focus.[56]

Walk the talk and then talk the walk!

Paul warns in Romans 8:7-11, a believer can live according to the flesh with the result of **death** (see James 1:13-15), or else live by the renewed spirit and mind, so as to experience **life.** The **resolution** of the intense warfare described in Romans 7, as well as the **inward harmony** and **peace** that result from **yielding to God.** Living according to the Spirit is God's will is for all of His children (see v. 1).

STUDY GUIDE: CHAPTER 9

1. Many young people feel that to express _____ will put them in dire straits with the church seniors. PG. 83

2. Young people are dissatisfied with the old wineskin of _____. PG. 83

3. This generation is not _____ minded but is _____ _____. PG. 83

4. The past several years have witnessed _____ _____ _____ the conflicts remain unresolved. PG. 83

5. _____ _____ is the kingdom of this world's greatest evil. PG. 84

6. Secular humanists do not believe _____ exists. PG. 84

7. To the humanists human beings are _____ and therefore no sexual acts should be considered improper. PG 84

8. Humanists put their trust in _____ rather than _____ _____. PG. 87

9. Our younger segments of the population have grown accustomed to _____ in our _____ _____. PG. 88

10. Why is the retention of those ages 18-29 years old so important to the church? Explain (PG. 88):

CHAPTER 10

FIRST IS HOLINESS THEN LOVE

Is it possible that we have left God out of Christianity? In the preceding chapters I have attempted to show that if not careful much of the American Church will be taken captive by the prevailing culture in faith and practice. The secular element and religious Christianity are working very subtly as they strive to remove the finished work of Christ, true worship and the gospel of grace from public view. They continue to present so-called other ways to God and at the same time push their agenda to neutralize the true God by elevating man to god status. Their progress is reflected not only in recent polls, but also in the rapidly falling state of morality in our society.

In spite of Barna's and others' reports showing that 75 plus percent of American adults describe their religious orientation as Christian; when applied to biblical standards and worldview many fall short. As the younger generation takes over the church many are creating their own biblical concepts of ministry. In an earlier chapter I pointed out that the younger generation is weary of the hypocrisy of their parents' generation and craving authenticity along with genuine transformation. Yet like their parents' generation, for many the focus remains on us and our activities rather than on God and His work of grace in Jesus Christ.

In all of these approaches, there is a tendency to want His love, but on our own personal terms. Even our preaching of the gospel tends to lean toward accessing God as a just another resource. What a self-deception! The answer to the question I asked in the beginning of this chapter points to two very unhealthy scenarios for the American church:

- The satanic attack on the truth of God's Word has intensified to a point where the issues are no longer just black or white, but today a culturally injected **gray area parading as truth** has been introduced and has infiltrated all of this nation's major institutions of government, education, the sciences and through the kingdom of this world's secular humanism trying to conform the church with their religious Christianity, secular philosophies of evolution, atheism, amorality, the new tolerance, and relativism.

- Secular humanism's indoctrination has made inroads in the public school systems, colleges and universities and will certainly attempt to influence the truth of God's Word in the next generation's faith and practices. The local churches must counter these threats with the truths of God's Word today! Thank God most American adults have not succumbed along with a great percentage of young people who are not accepting the devil's very subtle promotion of humanism and hedonism. As I stated in an earlier section, God is raising up faithful ministers to counter Satan's moves in the next generation, however, to be highly effective these ministers must be taught [now!] the truths of God's Word and a viable biblical worldview.

In order to stop Satan's invasion the leadership must bring the people back to the New Testament Church where holiness and the truths of God's Word are taught under the guidance and anointing of the Holy Spirit.

God's Holiness, His Wrath, and His Love

We hear it said even among some religious Christians and their gray area counsel, "God is love and surly he will not send anyone to hell." "He loves all men." "Not only that, God is good!" "He only gives good gifts!" *The truth of the matter is the holiness of God and the sinfulness of humans are in direct opposition to each other.* The holiness of God cannot tolerate humans' sinfulness; therefore demands that their sinfulness be exposed and judged. The reaction of God's holiness to humanity's sinfulness is wrath. If God did not deal with this sinfulness, then His law, His throne of holiness, His righteousness and justice would be in jeopardy. Only as sin is dealt with is God's character vindicated. Notice the following Scriptures which speak clearly of the wrath of God.

- "The Law brings about wrath" (see Romans 4:15).

- ". . . . He who does not believe the Son shall not see life; but the wrath of God abides on him" (see John 3:36).
- "For the wrath of God is revealed from heaven against all ungodliness and of unrighteousness of men . . . ." (see Romans 1:18).
- ". . . Hide us from the face of Him who sits on the throne, and from the wrath of the Lamb, for the great day of His wrath is come . . ." (see Revelation 6:16-17).

God's Wrath and Holiness

The wrath of God is the righteous reaction of a holy God against sin. However, in full view the Scripture shows that:

- Divine wrath **is not always executed immediately against sin**—because of **divine grace** and other moral attributes in the nature of God.
- This restrained wrath is waiting for God to provide a means for humankind to escape the wrath.

God was not caught in the dark when Adam sinned. The Scripture clearly states that before the foundation of the world God's answer was Jesus Christ (John 17:5, 24). The plan of redemption was already realized. Man broke God's holy law, violating the principles of righteousness by his **willful disobedience.** This brought all of humanity under the power of sin and made his conscious heavy with guilt:

- God in His holiness must execute His wrath and judgment upon Adam's sin.
- With the violation of God's divine law came the divine penalty of death (Genesis 2:17). God's wrath must be appeased!
- The law demanded satisfaction and that could only be satisfied when its standard of holiness could be upheld. Not until the death penalty had been executed (Romans 6:23) upon sin could the law be satisfied, **God's holiness and**

> **righteousness upheld** (see Ezekiel 18:4, 29; Hebrews 9:27). Sin had to be purged!
> - Sin had to be appeased before there could be any reconciliation between God and humankind. The appeasement is the atonement![57]
> - This "atonement" means the covering, the expiation, the satisfaction, the appeasement, or the reconciliation. This word encompasses all redemptive words.

It is this wrath that needed the appeasement before a holy God and a sinful human being could **ever** be reconciled. The word atonement means **"to be made one"** (see Exodus 29:33-37; Leviticus 16:6-17).

God's Wrath and Love

In the first section of this chapter, I spoke about how many in our culture have their damaging views about God. The media assists the culture by helping to distort the true reality of biblical Christianity. These ideals picture Him as a Santa Claus, just another resource. One who supplies your needs; because He is rich and loves all humankind. Further some think that there are many ways to God. Again, these thoughts are even believed by some so-called religious Christians. From the last section, we saw that human beings have a distinct problem. That problem has to do with the totally-ordered moral attributes of God.

These attributes are the very nature and being of God, as holiness and love [in that order]. The Bible reveals that **God is holy** (1 Peter 1:16) and **God is love** (1 John 4:16). As I stated earlier these attributes are perfectly ordered in God:

- In His love, God desired to save the sinner.
- In His holiness, God must execute His wrath and judgment upon the sin.
- How could this be done? God could not manifest love at the expense of His holiness—neither could God save the sinner without judgment upon the sin! What could He do?

Is the Holy Spirit framing this predicament up for you?

- Unless God moves humanity will be eternally separated from Him. God makes His move!
- Remember, Calvary **is not first** a revelation of the love of God—but **is first** a revelation of the holiness of God.

God's order is **always** holiness, and then love—for God's love can **never** be revealed at the expense of God's holiness.

- The same apostle John who speaks of *"the love of God"* is the same one who speaks of *"the wrath of God"* (John 3:16, 17, 36). He speaks of *"the blood of the Lamb"* as well as *"the wrath of the Lamb"* and yet it is *"the same redemptive Lamb"* (Revelation 5:9-10; 6:16-17).
- Saints in both the Old and New Testaments experienced and retained this order.

  1. Moses received the revelation of the Lord God in the burning bush. Notice, it was holiness first, then Israel's redemption (see Exodus 3:5, 9-10).
  2. Isaiah received a revelation of God's holiness first, then the call to the prophetic office (see Isaiah 6:1-6).
  3. Paul spoke of the wrath of God against man's sinfulness before he even mentioned the love of God in Christ (Romans 1:118; 2:5, 8; 4:15; 5:5).

It is noteworthy to see that the theme of the Epistles to the Romans is that of justification and the reconciliation of humankind to God. However, in Romans 1-3 the emphasis is on the wrath of a holy and righteous God revealed against all ungodliness and sin. The subject of love is not expressly brought up until Romans 5:5.

How can God in love save the sinner without violating His holiness and executing His wrath upon sin? The answer is found in the atonement, typified in the Old Testament:

- In the Old Testament the offerer brought the sacrificial lamb **without blemish** to the priest.
- He laid his hands on the head of the animal signifying the **transfer** of his sins and his family's sins to the sacrificial animal.
- Nothing is said concerning the offerer, but emphasis concerns the sacrifice; which had to meet standards [without blemish] set by God not the priests.
- Notice this whole process leaves the entire outcome to the *sacrifice* if acceptable it provided a covering for the offerer's sin. This was repeated annually. God permitted this to go on for 1500 years providing an action picture of the Lamb of God's **once and for all** sacrifice which was prophesied of in the Law, the Psalms and the Prophets—and then fulfilled in the work of the Lord Jesus Christ.[58] Whereas the sins of the Old Testament offerer were covered for one year, however, Christ was offered **once** for the sins of the entire world [There will never, ever be another need for a sacrifice]. For those who receive this atoning work of Christ by faith have scripturally, experienced the "new birth" and are "in Him." We are a new creation; He took our sins and gave us His righteousness (see 2 Corinthians 5:17, 21)!

In brief review of an earlier section and more in this chapter, at the new birth you receive new life in your spirit which has been quickened by the Holy Spirit (see John 3:3; 14:17). Additionally, your born again spirit is sealed from sin by the Holy Spirit. **Knowing this** what Christian would want to continue in sin? God deserves our highest love and praise. While we were yet sinners, Christ died for us! However, we must remember that our soul and body must be renewed by the Spirit and the truths of God's Word in sanctification. Sin in the Christian's life opens the door for the devil. That's pure misery, but 1 John 1:9 reveals that you are to repent immediately, confess that sin, and get forgiveness [which is already resident in your spirit] once forgiveness comes forward the devil has to go and you move forward in "the faith"(see Jude 3).

God's Wrath and Christ

In the atoning work of the Lord Jesus Christ, God deals in holiness with sin—and in love with the sinner. In the work of the cross, holiness and love are seen in perfect balance. God judging sin and making provision for the sinner's salvation—Christ was made an offering for our sin (Isaiah 53:3-6; II Corinthians 5:21; Romans 3:25; I Peter 2:24; 3:18). Paul summarizes the view of Christ's death when he says: **"Christ died for our sins according to the Scriptures"** (I Corinthians 15:3-4).

Study the accompanying Scriptures for a through understanding of the atonement:

- The death of Christ was part of God's eternal purpose. (Rev. 13:8; 1 Peter 1:18-20; Acts 2:22-23).
- The death of Christ was foretold under the Law, Psalms and Prophets. (Luke 24:27, 44-45; Matthew 5:17-18; 11:13).
- The death of Christ was the chief purpose of the Incarnation. (Mark 10:45; Hebrews 2:9, 14; 9:26; 1 John 3:5; Matthew 20:28). He was born to be crucified.
- The death of Christ is the major theme of the **Gospel of grace.** (1 Corinthians 15:1-4; Romans 5:5-10, 12-21) Christ died for our sins. The death penalty was paid. This is God's good news to all sinners.
- The death of Christ is essential to Christianity. All world religions are built upon the teachings of their founders, who are dead or will die. Christianity **alone** is built upon the **death** and **resurrection of Jesus Christ,** its founder. Without the death and resurrection of Christ, Christianity is reduced to the level of just "another" religion.
- The death of Christ is essential to our salvation. (John 3:14-15; 12:24; Romans 3:25-26; Matthew 16:21; Mark 8:31; Luke 9:22; 17:25; Acts 17:3; 1 Peter 3:18; Matthew 20:28; 26:28; Luke 22:19; 1 Timothy 2:6; II Corinthians 5:14; 1 Peter 2:24; Hebrews 8:28; 1 John 3:5). It was necessary that Christ die, for God cannot pardon sinners unless sin is dealt with. In order for God to pardon sinners and remain consistent with

His holiness **Christ must pay sin's penalty.** The wages of sin is death.

- The death of Christ was a voluntary Act. (John 10:17-18; Matthew 26:53-54; Isaiah 53:12). The cross was Christ's deliberate choice, not His fate. He offered Himself a freewill or "voluntary offering" as shadowed forth in the **voluntary burnt, meal and peace offerings** in Leviticus 1-3.[59]

What seemed to be Christ's tragedy was God's triumph!

- The death of Christ is prominent in the New Testament Writings. (I Corinthians 2:2; 15:1-4; Galatians 1:4; 2:20; 6:14; Romans 5:6; I Thessalonians 4:14; Philippians 3:10; Ephesians 2:13; Colossians 1:14; I Timothy 2:6; I Peter 1:11-12; I John 3:1-4; Hebrews 9:26; Hebrews 9:26; Revelations 5:1-13).

Because of who Jesus is and what He has accomplished in His life and death—the death of Christ is of infinite and eternal value. Jesus was God incarnate, the eternal Son of God and it is this which makes His death of eternal and therefore infinite value. His death conquered all other deaths.

The Scriptures also say that Christ descended into the lower parts of the earth and led captivity captive (Ephesians 4:8-10). So Christ led captivity captive after His triumphant victory over Satan, and spoiled principalities and powers. He conquered sin, sickness, disease, the curse, demons and death, all of which had a hold on humanity. Thus Christ led this "captivity captive" (see Judges5:12; Job 42:10; Psalm 68:18, 126:1). At the close of the three days and nights, Jesus returned to the earth in His resurrected and glorified body.[60]

Christ and the Resurrection

The resurrection of Jesus Christ is one of the great **fundamental doctrines of the Christian faith.** There are more than one hundred references to the resurrection of Christ in the New Testament. Many people believe in the death of Christ—yet *reject* His resurrection. However, both of these facts are declared by the same writer. Paul found it inconceivable that he should be condemned for believing in the resurrection! He questioned, "Why should it be thought incredible by you that God raises the dead? (see Acts 26:8; Romans 4:25).

The death and resurrection of Christ should **never** be separated for one preceded the other—and the one completes the other. A balanced Gospel always includes His saving death and His saving resurrection life. In Romans 5:10 Paul says, *"For If when we were enemies we were reconciled to God through the death* [blood] *of His Son, much more, having been reconciled, we shall be saved by His life."*

When we were God's enemies, Christ was able by His blood to reconcile us to God. Certainly now that we are God's children, the Savior can keep us by His living grace.

The New Testament

The New Testament clearly reveals that the Old Testament **foreshadowed** the **atoning work of Christ in** [the Tabernacle of Moses]. Some forty chapters of Scripture are dedicated to this subject. The Book of Hebrews especially deals with the atoning sacrifices and emphasizes the Day of Atonement ceremony. Jesus Christ being both Priest and Sacrifice fulfills in Himself the Day of Atonement ceremonies:

- He offered the sacrifice at Calvary's cross, the New Testament's sacrificial altar.
- His body was broken and His blood was shed there.
- In His ascension He entered within the veil of the heavenly and the true sanctuary.
- There He presented Himself and His blood, at the throne of God, the New Testament Ark of the Covenant.

- He Himself is also the mercy-seat (see Hebrews 6:19-20; Matthew 27:51; Hebrews 9:1-28; 10:5:22; 13:11-15, 20; Revelation 11:19; 15:5).

The Apostle Paul says of Christ: "Whom God hath set forth to be a propitiation (Greek "Hilasteerion" or "Mercy Seat") through faith in His blood[61] . . . ." (Romans 3:25). <u>The Atonement is the actual and official presentation of the blood of Jesus Christ at the throne of God by Himself, our Great High Priest.</u>" This is the atonement, the reconciliation, and the finished work of Christ (see John 17:1-4; 19:30).

What then are the results of Christ's finished work?

1. The sins of the believer are cleansed, not just covered (see 1 John 1:5-7).
2. The believer is accepted of God in Christ's righteousness (see II Corinthians 5:19-21).
3. God's wrath is appeased, He is pacified, His Law is vindicated (see Romans 1:18; 2:5; 5:9).
4. God is gracious, propitiated towards sinful people (see Luke 18:13; Hebrews 9:5; I John 2:2; 4:10; Romans 3:25).
5. Reconciliation has taken place! God and humankind face each other *in* Christ (see Hebrews 2:17).
6. The believer has a blood-sprinkled mercy seat in the throne of God by which he or she can approach God (see Romans 3:25; Hebrews 4:16).
7. Christ is our Great High Priest and lives in the power of an endless life (see Hebrews 7:16).
8. The blood of Jesus Christ is ever available for cleansing; the believer is brought to a state of sinless perfection (see I John 1:5-7; Revelation 12:11; Hebrews 7:11).

Without a doubt the greatest illustration of the Doctrine of the Atonement [Grace] is that which God provided to Israel in the Tabernacle of Moses. In the Outer Court, at the Brazen Altar, the Israelites would see in the sacrificial victims the great truths of redemption, ransom, substitution, and propitiation. In the Most Holy

Place, at the Ark of the Covenant, especially on the great Day of Atonement, **the great truths** of reconciliation and atonement would be seen as the High Priest made the actual and official presentation of **the atoning blood** on the mercy seat. And then over and above the whole of the economy would be seen—**the revelation of God's Law and wonderful GRACE.**

STUDY GUIDE: CHAPTER 10

1. _____% of American adults describes their religious orientation as Christian. PG. 97

2. The younger generation is _____ of the _____ of their parents' generation. PG. 97

3. Younger people are craving _____. PG. 97

4. God demands that the sinfulness of humans be _____ and _____. PG. 98

5. The _____ of God is the reaction of a holy God against sin. PG. 98

6. The wrath of God is the _____ of a Holy God. PG. 98

7. Calvary is always first a revelation of _____ and the revelation of _____. PG. 99

8. Christ offered Himself as a _____ or _____ _____ offering. PG. 98

9. The resurrection of Jesus Christ is one of the great _____ _____ of the faith. PG. 98

10. The _____ and _____ of Christ should never be separated for one preceded the other. PG. 98

11. The Old Testament Tabernacle foreshadowed the _____ of _____ PG. 99

12. The _____ of _____ is ever available for _____ the _____. PG. 100

13. The _____ is the actual and official _____ of the _____ of Jesus Christ. PG. 102

14. The blood of Jesus Christ is ever _____ for the _____ the believer. PG. 103

15. Explain the contrast of sin and other truths of God's Word concerning the Old Testament and the New Testament sacrificial Lamb, Christ PG. 102-3):

CHAPTER 11

VICTORY THROUGH PERSONAL HOLINESS

Recently as I sat watching the 700 Club, on one news segment, a little seven year old Egyptian girl walking down a Cairo street was shot in the chest and died. In an interview with her parents, both Coptic Christians, there was no anger, threats or pleading for justice. They expressed no animosity toward the shooter, who was still at large, but said they were praying for him. On another newscast a few days later another mother in this city, thousands of miles from Cairo Egypt, lost her son to a shooter as he was shot while standing in the front yard of the family home. She praised God right there on camera, with all of the anguish and pain. Like the couple in Egypt, she prayed for the killer of her baby. The shooter was still at large.

I heard a story the other day out of China wherein a pastor from America asked some people in one of the underground churches if they wanted him to pray for them, one individual piped up, "You pray for us? All the American church is about are things, politics and money." No! No! We are praying for you!" He continues one third of us are in prison, we are shunned, persecuted and beaten but through it all we have the victory. In the midst of it all, Christ is faithful and with us. All we have is Jesus, our only hope! We are going to make it. There is absolutely no reason to doubt these people are not true believers—they know and love Jesus, **personal holiness!**

The very mention of holiness in many church circles brings on either a snicker or a hearty Amen! Many consider themselves holy based on their personal knowledge and definition of the word. Holiness has been defined by individuals and denominations in many ways. When we notice its usage in the Bible, the definition many people are spouting as the true holiness is not biblical at all, but a concoction of men.

"Holiness is the fruit not the root of salvation!"

Like all other concepts of God and the things of God, we must look to the Word of God for truth. It has been said, the Old Testament is the dictionary for the New Testament. I like that saying because of the way the drama unfolds bringing forth an actual picture, in this case of true holiness. The vivid example of holiness is found in the burning bush episode with Moses.

Turn and See

In the Scripture passage Moses said, *"I will now turn aside and see this great sight, why the bush does not burn." So when the Lord saw that he had turned aside to look, God called to him from the midst of the bush and said, "Moses, Moses!" And he said, "Here I am." Then He said, "Do not draw near this place. Take your sandals off your feet, for the place where you stand is holy ground"* (Exodus 3:3-5).

Moses had shepherded his sheep in that section of the desert for years, no doubt moving them right by that same bush on the same ground. It was just like the rest of the desert then, how can it be holy ground now and not then? If Moses had reached down and scooped up a hand full of sand and walked twenty paces back over the ground he had just walked on and compared the two grounds; the sand there would have been the same as that in his hand. Why did the Lord declare the ground to be holy?

It was holy ground because God said it was holy! Why, because He had *separated* it as the spot of desert where He would reveal Himself to Moses. So in essence all the rest of the desert remained unholy. If God had moved the meeting four miles east of that spot then that piece of ground would have been just as holy. Holiness then means separated from one thing and separated to another. Throughout the Old and New Testaments, the root word holy is translated into such terms as set apart, dedicated, consecrated, sanctified, and saint. Whatever their particular usage in the Bible, each is rooted in the concept of separateness. Until the Lord set that particular part of the desert apart from the rest of the desert, He could not call it holy. For a person to become holy in this sense he or she must *depart* from anything unholy, or holiness is impossible. However, that that is separated must become reconnected:

- *United* or *devoted to something else.*
- *New practices must be added to your life to replace the old patterns.*
- *We abandon our unholy ways and pursue His holy ways.*

Without both aspects of this separation, biblical holiness is not possible. The believer must flee from something and then follow after something else. We find these two demonstrated in 2 Timothy 2:22:

Flee [separate yourself **from**] *also youthful lusts; but pursue* [separate yourself **to**] *righteousness, faith, love, peace with those who call on the Lord **out of a pure heart.***[62]

Again, we must seek to fulfill the whole of righteousness. Pursuing righteousness or any of the other fruit mentioned above cannot be obtained without fleeing youthful lusts, and not only sexual immorality, but also such *lusts* as pride, desire for wealth and power for unbiblical purposes, jealousy, self-assertiveness, and an argumentative spirit. Imbalance and error in this matter will eventually shipwreck your life.

But personal holiness occurs when we leave behind the patterns of this world in order to become more Christlike in our character and conduct [development of the fruit of the Spirit]. The apostle Peter wrote:

*But as He who called you is holy, you also be holy in all your conduct, because it is written, **"Be holy, for I am holy."*** (1 Peter 1:15-16).

Holiness essentially defines the Christian's *new nature* and *conduct* in contrast with his or her pre-salvation lifestyle. The reason for practicing a holy manner of living is that Christians are associated with the holy God and must treat Him and His Word with respect and reverence. We therefore glorify Him best by being like Him.

Verse 17 begins, *If you call on the Father.* This is another way of saying, "If you are a Christian."

- Holiness is the center of God's will for you.
- The Father wants you to be holy.
- The believer who knows God and that He judges the works of all His children fairly will respect God, our heavenly Father.
- May you depart from all that is unholy and pursue all that is holy.

Discipline toward Holiness

Anthropology, the study of man has shown that every known culture in the world honors some form of holiness. Certain places and practices are described as "sacred" while others are called "taboo." Both of these positions describe separation from that which is secular to that which is sacred.

I read a story some time ago concerning a man who had completed the tedious task of painting his barn. Proud of his work, he boasted about how white and beautiful his barn was and had to be the most truly beautiful white in the county. That night it snowed; as he started his day, he headed out to look at his beautiful barn. He was shocked his barn appeared to be more of a light shade of gray against the backdrop of the beautiful white snow which had blanketed the area during the night.

Like the painter, we to are deceived thinking more highly of ourselves then we ought to think. Until we come to see ourselves as God sees us our very nature will grow worse. The tendency to try bringing God down to our level or convince ourselves that He does not exist has greatly widened the gap between heaven and humanity. This depravity has negatively affected our thinking and has demonically charged the environment around us.

The Scripture reveals that the sudden realization of Isaiah personal depravity came like a heart attack from heaven upon his feeble being as he had his vision of the holiness of God. His pain-filled cry,

"Woe is me!
for I am undone;
because I am a man
of unclean lips;
and I dwell in the midst
of a people of unclean lips;
for mine eyes have seen the King,
the Lord of hosts,"

Again, until we have seen ourselves, as God see us:

- We will not be disturbed over the demonically distorted conditions in people around us as long as they do not rock the boat and upset our comfort zones.
- We are learning to live with uncleanness as we allow the culture to conform us to a secular worldview that incorporates their mandates on the new tolerance, same sex marriages, co-habitation and illegitimacy as natural and to be expected.
- We are no longer disappointed in unfaithful politicians, and secular humanistic orientated professor and teachers.
- We are satisfied with containing our problems, rather than solving them.

Like the painter, we are constructing what we think is the true meaning of divine holiness. We actually know nothing like true divine holiness. Scripturally it stands apart, unique and unattainable. Like all other spiritual matters, the natural man or woman, boy or girl is blind and cannot comprehend it.

Only the Holy Spirit can impart to the human spirit the knowledge of the true holiness of God; therefore we can know by grace through faith which comes by hearing, and hearing by the Word of God." Through revelation of God in the Scriptures and the illumination of the Spirit of truth the believer gains everything and loses nothing.

Holiness is God's Way

Holy is the way of God. To be holy He does not conform to a certain standard—He is the standard! Because He is holy, His attributes are holy; which means everything belonging to Him must be thought of as holy. The English word holy is derived from the Anglo-Saxon *halig, hal,* meaning "well, whole."

So, God's first concern for His universe holiness the moral condition necessary for proper health. Sin is temporary, a moral sickness making a bump in the road that ultimately will end in death. We can conclude then, whatever is contrary and threatens His standard of that health [holiness] must be dealt with.

God is holy with an absolute holiness, which He cannot impart to humans. However, there is a relative holiness which He has made available to His children on earth through the blood of the Lamb, **and He requires it of them.** He has said to His church, *"Be holy, for I am holy."* The holiness, wrath and health of the creation work in tandem and are inseparable. Every wrathful judgment then is in actuality a holy **act of preservation.** We cannot ignore the solemn exhortation from God's word, *"Follow peace with all men, and* **holiness,** *without which no man shall see God,"* Above all we must believe that through grace, God sees us perfect in His Son while He chastens and purges us that we may be partakers of His holiness. Holiness is the way!

STUDY GUIDE: CHAPTER 11

1. The very mention of holiness in many _____ circles brings either a _____ or a hearty amen. PG. 104

2. How could the ground upon which Moses stood be declared holy?
    Explain:

3. To be holy we must depart from anything that is _____. PG. 105

4. Personal holiness happens when we become more _____. PG. 105

5. Until we see ourselves as _____ _____ us our nature will grow worse. PG. 106

6. The believer revelation of God through the _____ and the _____ of the Holy Spirit. PG. 107

7. The natural man is _____ and cannot _____ holiness. PG 107

8. Biblical holiness is derived from an Anglo-Saxon word meaning _____ or _____. PG. 107

9. God is holy with _____ _____. PG. 107

10. Holiness that God imparts is through the _____ of _____. PG 107

11. Without _____ no man shall see God. PG. 107

12. God sees us _____ in His Son and He _____ and purges us. PG. 107

SECTION IV

GRACE IS SPIRITUAL

CHAPTER 12

Grace Walk

Because we are in the kingdom of God and totally dependent upon Him, we have a grace-given duty to demonstrate visibly and tangibly as *salt* and *light*. Thus, we are to make life palatable showing others the narrow way through living out the *revealed truths* of God's Word. As the Church of the Living God, we are sent out into the total of society as ambassadors of Christ's kingdom as His *living grace* to serve some useful purpose for the good of others. We must never forget, the church is always *fallible* and always liable to correction from God's *infallible* revelation. The truths of God's Word must be rediscovered and defended afresh in *each* generation.

Grace Alone, in Christ Alone, through Faith Alone

All Christians think of Jesus as necessary. However most don't trust themselves to interpret the Word of God, the Bible. Many turn to second-hand means, books, or others for interpretation; in this case the final authority to them is based on others and not necessarily based on solid doctrine. Within the past thirty years, reasons for Christ have grown from His being a teacher to a life coach, but as the Lamb of God who takes away the sins of the world He is basically unknown. Because so few **know** they are lost, they really don't think they need to be saved from the wrath of God. Their attitude says, "If I am not lost—I don't need to be found."

Many Christians living in our society today rely totally upon themselves to solve all of life's problems hurled at them, not realizing that we were not created to live that way. Christ, our example was totally dependent upon the Father while here on the earth, therefore we are to be totally dependent upon Him through the power of the Holy Spirit.

We also need to be aware of the fact that there are many people in the local churches practicing *religious* Christianity, which is not based on the faith and practices of biblical principles and promises of God. Religious Christianity directs its faith toward the doctrines, concepts and practices of men; which can not pass the test for true biblical teachings.

This non-biblical type of Christianity has caused much confusion through the years. Even more importantly it causes thousands of people to miss being born again into the kingdom of God; and therefore, they miss heaven!

Unfortunately in today's *religious environment* it is easy for people to get involved in what may be called Christianity—but which does not necessarily mean a commitment to Jesus Christ and His teachings. There is an enormous difference. It is very easy to be involved; as involvement only requires activity. People are committed to a vast array of different ideas and philosophies. They can even be doing many works in the name of Jesus, but that does not necessarily mean they have experienced a personal relationship with Jesus Christ and are spiritually born again into the kingdom of God.

All Christians must be committed to Jesus Christ and His teachings as found in the Scriptures. As Christians we must know **what** we believe and **why** we believe it. This is possible only as each Christian comes into the knowledge of the *revealed* truths of God's Word for themselves. This is a necessary condition to be met if we are to be *true* salt and light in the world reflecting the *Son* of God. Additionally, the Christian must be led by the Holy Spirit to the knowledge that the **Bible alone**, from Genesis to Revelation is God's unfolding story of His eternal purpose to glorify Himself in the salvation of humankind that comes only through Jesus Christ. So salvation comes to us by **grace alone** in **Christ alone,** through **faith alone.**

Through proper hearing and application of the gospel a person will see the need to be rescued from a situation that is totally hopeless and impossible to achieve in their own natural strength and abilities. The Bible announces the kind of rescue he or she needs and the gospel provides the means [Christ alone bearing our sins and guilt on Calvary].

All of our salvation is found in Christ alone—none in ourselves!

The Gospel is **not** Christ plus:

- Our spiritual disciplines
- Our free will
- Our acts of mercy and love
- Our acts of service to others
- Our spiritual experiences
- Our gifts and callings
- Our station and surroundings

An understanding of God's righteousness reminds us that a sinner must be judged. The apostle Paul writes, *"For in the righteousness of God is revealed from faith to faith; as it is written, the just shall live by faith"* (Romans 1:17). God judges us not only by His righteousness, but with His righteousness imputed to our account. The doctrine of justification by grace alone through faith alone was *recovered.* When a person first exercises faith in Christ and:

- Gives up their own claims of righteousness,
- And gives up their struggles for divine approval,
- He or she is saved from the penalty of sin and declared righteous.

As the believer lives by faith, God continues to save him or her from the power of sin to live righteously. The New Testament speaks of salvation in the:

- Past tense—in the past the believer has been saved from the **penalty** of sin (Ephesians 2:8).
- Present tense—in the present, the believer is being saved from the **power** of sin (see 2 Corinthians 2:15).
- Future tense—in the future, the believer will be saved from the very **presence** of sin (see Romans 13:11).

Thus justification is not something the believer has to wait for until the end of life, but is declared at the beginning of the Christian life. In other words, salvation is by grace alone through faith alone in Christ alone.

The gospel is the only message that reveals to us the sovereignty of God, the holiness of God, and the purity of God as revealed in the gospel. The statement: *"the just shall live by faith"* was true in the Old Testament times (see Habakkuk 2:4) just as sure as it is true in this **Age of Grace.** God has always dealt in faith and through faith:

- By faith Abel offered also a blood sacrifice.
- By faith Enoch walked with God.
- By faith Noah built an ark.
- By faith Abraham moved out into a strange country, not knowing where he was going—but moving by faith.
- By faith Moses chose to suffer the afflictions of God's people rather than be called the son of Pharaoh's daughter (study Hebrews 11).

Jesus said to His disciples, *"Have faith in God"* (Mark 11:22). The gospel of Grace reveals to us that we live by grace through faith—not by sight, not by might, nor by feelings.

The devil hates the gospel of Grace and is doing everything in his limited power to discredit the *fundamentals of the faith* and bring Jesus down to the human level of thinking. The devil has used Hollywood movies, the media and any other means to make Jesus just a good man and teacher. We begin to treat faith as if it is our contribution. Others do not seem to be bothered by God's justice and wrath, as if He was too nice to judge or they are too good to deserve a sentence. We believe:

- That justification wherein Christ's righteousness is imputed to the sinner.
- That in regeneration the sinner's spirit is quickened by the Holy Spirit.
- That in adoption the sinner is adopted back into the family of God.

These are simultaneous in the experience of sinner obtained upon the condition of salvation by grace through faith in the finished work of Jesus Christ, preceded by repentance and to this precious truth we have the three-fold witness of God's Word; the Holy Spirit; and the human spirit:[63]

The Witness of God's Word

In order to safeguard these truths of assurance of our personal salvation, we will examine the witness of God's Word.

1. *The Assurance of Pardon*

"Let the wicked forsake his way, and the unrighteous man his thoughts: and let him return to the Lord, and He will have mercy upon him; and to our God, for He will abundantly pardon" (Isaiah 55:7). "He that covers his sins shall not prosper: but whoso confesses and forsakes them shall have mercy" (Proverbs 28:13). "If we confess our sins, He is faithful and just to forgive us our sins, and to cleanse us from all unrighteousness" (I John 1:9).

2. *The Assurance of Acceptance*

"Come unto Me, all you that labor and are heavy laden, and I will give you rest" (Matthew 11:28). "The one who comes to Me I will by no means cast out" (John 6:37). "There is therefore now no condemnation to those who are in Christ Jesus" (Romans 8:1).

3. *The Assurance of Salvation*

"That if you confess with your mouth the Lord Jesus and believe in your heart that God has raised Him from the dead, you will be saved. For with the heart one believes unto righteousness, and with the mouth confession is made unto salvation. Or the Scripture says, "Whoever believes on Him will not be put to shame. For "whoever calls on the name of the Lord shall be saved" (Romans 10:9-11, 13).

4. *The Assurance of Sonship*

"But as many as received Him, to them He gave the right to become children of God, to those who believe in His name: who were born, not of blood, nor of the will of the flesh, nor of the will of man, but of God" (John 1:12-13).

5. *The Assurance of Eternal Life*

"Most assuredly, I say to you, he who hears My word and believes in Him who sent Me has everlasting life, and shall not come into judgment, but has passed from death into life" (John 5:24). "If we receive the witness of men, the witness of God is greater; for this is the witness of God which He has testified of His Son. He who believes in the Son of God has the witness in himself; he who does not believe God has made Him a liar, because he has not believed the testimony that God has given of His Son. And this is the testimony: that God has given us eternal life, and this life is in His Son. He who has the Son has life; he who does not have the Son of God, that you may know that you have eternal life, and that you may continue to believe in the name of the Son of God" (I John 5:9-11).

6. *The Assurance of God's Continued Favor*

"But if we walk in the light as He is in the light, we have fellowship with one another, and the blood of Jesus Christ His Son cleanses us from all sin" (1 John 1:7). And you, who once were alienated and enemies in your mind by wicked works, yet now He has reconciled in the body of His flesh through death, to present you holy, and blameless, and above reproach in His sight—if indeed you continue in the faith, grounded and steadfast, and are not moved away from the hope of the gospel . . . . As you therefore have received Christ Jesus the Lord, so walk in Him" (Colossians 1:21-23; 2:6).

The Witness of the Holy Spirit

In addition to the objective witness of God's Word—there is the subjective witness of the Spirit. "Now he who keeps His commandments abides in Him, and He in him [or her]" (1 John 1:24). "By this we know that we abide in Him, and He in us, because He has given us His Spirit" (1 John 4:13). These passages are not objective witnesses, but they refer to an internal [I know] assurance deep within the human consciousness. The New Testament sets forth three examples to present this inner testimony of the Spirit of God:

1. *The Seal of the Spirit*

In II Corinthians 1:22 we read, "Who also has *sealed* us and given us the Spirit in our hearts [spirits] as a guarantee." We go to a Notary Public to have our documents notarized. Once signed he or she employs a seal authenticating what was thereby sealed. The Holy Spirit in the believer's life is the divine seal upon that life. "The Lord knows those who are His," and, "Let everyone who names the name of Christ depart from iniquity" (2 Timothy 2:19). The seal of the Holy Spirit is assurance to the believer and a sign or witness to the world.

2. *The Earnest of the Spirit*

In commercial agreements the *earnest* is a down or partial payment which binds the deal obligating both parties to complete the transaction. The Holy Spirit is the earnest or down payment of the infinite blessings God plans to give us in heaven. O what a guarantee and foretaste of heaven we have in walking in the Spirit.

> "And this is eternal life,
> that they may know You,
> the only true God,
> and
> Jesus Christ
> whom you have sent" (John 17:3).

3. *The Testimony of the Spirit*

"And because you are sons, God has sent forth the Spirit of His Son into your hearts, crying out, "Abba, Father!" (Galatians 4:6). "The Spirit Himself bears witness with our spirit that we are children of God" (Romans 8:16). By the Spirit of adoption the pardoned sinner is enabled to look up to God and say, "Father!"

The Witness of the Human Spirit

To the direct witness of the Holy Spirit there is added the indirect witness of our own spirits. The Spirit of God bears witness *along with our spirits.* There is a joint witness of His Spirit and mine that I have passed from condemnation to acceptance and sonship. This indirect witness confirms the direct, assuring me that I am not presuming upon God. Within my own consciousness I perceive that I am a new creature, that old things have passed away and all things and all things have become new. This I know if I am born of the Spirit.

To the man born blind the Pharisees put questions he could not answer. But he could not be silenced. *"One thing I know,"* he said, *"that, whereas I was blind now I see"* (John 9:25). Praise God! A born again Christian has the same kind of indisputable evidence.

STUDY GUIDE: CHAPTER 12

1. We are to be _____ and _____ making life palatable for others. PG. 111

2. Like Christ our example we are to be _____ _____ upon Him as He was to the Father. PG. 111

3. Religious Christianity is not based on _____ _____ and the gospel of Christ. PG. 111

4. Salvation comes to us by _____ _____ in Christ alone, _____ _____ _____. PG 112

5. The New Testament speaks of salvation in three tenses. List the three tenses _____ _____ _____. PG. 112

6. The devil hates the _____ of _____. PG. 113

7. Satan does everything he can to _____ the fundamentals of faith. PG. 113

8. List two of the assurances of personal salvation: PG.113
   -
   -

9. Explain below "adoption" as referenced in salvation. PG. 115

10. The seal of the Holy Spirit is _____ to the believer. PG. 115

11. God's eternal purpose is to _____ Himself in the _____ of humankind that comes through Jesus Christ. PG. 114

A FINAL WORD SAVING GRACE TO YOU!

The truth of grace is now restored to the Church of God. All spiritual blessings are the result of **grace,** and grace is God's unmerited, unearned, undeserved favor toward us. There is absolutely nothing a man, woman, girl or boy can do, give, live, or be in order to merit grace.

Grace is bestowed upon believers because of our faith in the finished work of Jesus Christ.

Salvation is all of grace—without mixture. "And if by grace, then it is no more of works: But if it be of works, then is it no more grace: otherwise work is no more work" (see Romans 11:6). "In Christ Jesus" believers are established in grace. In Hebrews 13:1-9, the writer admonishes:

"Let brotherly love continue. Do not forget to entertain strangers, for by so doing some have unwittingly entertained angels. Remember the prisoners as if chained with them—those who are mistreated—since you yourselves are in the body also . . . . Let your conduct be without covetousness; be content with such things as you have. For He Himself has said, "I will never leave you nor forsake you." So we may boldly say: "The Lord is my helper; I will not fear. What can man do to me?"

*"Remember those who rule over you, who have spoken the word of God to you, whose faith follow, considering the outcome of their conduct. Jesus Christ is the same yesterday, today, and forever. Do not be carried about with various and strange doctrines. It is good that the **heart be established by grace,** not with foods which have not profited those who have been occupied with them."*

In the final chapter of the Book of Hebrews the writer focuses on some of the essential practical ethics of Christian living. These ethics are as essential for today as they were then; because they help

Christians to properly portray the gospel to the world and encourage others to believe in Christ, and therefore bringing glory to God:

- Love for fellow believers (v.1; see also John 13:35).
- Love those who are strangers (v. 2; see also Romans 12:13; 1 Timothy 3:2).
- Identify with the suffering with others because they also suffer physical "pain in the body and hardships" (v. 3).
- Honor marriage. God highly honors marriage between one man and one woman, which He instituted (v. 4; also see Genesis 2:24).
- Sexual activity in a marriage is pure, but any sexual activity outside of marriage God will judge. Though legislators the world over are establishing laws favoring same sex marriages, no-fault divorces and co-habitation, open homosexuality and lesbianism, the Bible has much to say on these subjects and none of it is favorable, God will judge. Remember, like Christ we hate the sin, but we are to love the sinner (Study Romans 1:24-32; Galatians 5:17-21; Ephesians 5:3-6).
- Let your conduct [walk] be without coveting and lusting after material riches which is the root of all kinds of evil, for which many have strayed away from the faith in their greediness (v. 5; see also 1 Timothy 6:10; 3:3).
- Be content with such things as you have [be bold and do not fear] and remember Jesus' promise, **"I will never leave you nor forsake you"** (see Hebrews 13:5-6).
- Remember those who rule over you [faithful leaders within the church] who:
    1) rule;
    2) speak the word of God; and
    3) establish the pattern of faith for the people to follow

    4) (Study carefully vv.7-9; Hebrews 11; Acts 20:28; 1Timothy 3:1-7; Titus 1:5-9).

The New Testament contains many warnings against false teaching and false teachers. The writer understands that those believers and believers today should be established by grace—not with rituals of the law such as abstaining from meats or rituals practiced under the Mosaic system. ***GRACE IS CHRIST*** and Christ in the heart of the believer is all-sufficient. There is absolutely nothing that can be added! God looks upon the heart, and when we serve Him with whole-hearted love, humility, and dedication we will eat right, drink right, and live right. Thus the Christian is *established with grace*—not with meats, dress, observance of days, or rituals. **Saving grace to you!**

God's Wonderful Grace Is Sufficient for Me

My soul is at peace as on-ward I trod, For I can re-ly on
The demons of hell their darts at the cast, I'll have no fear
And when I have sailed life's journey at last, And safe in
heav'n's harbor the promise of God, He gave me His word
when He set me free, My for He'll hold me fast; No harm
can be-fall while His face I see, His my an-chor is cast; The
theme of my praise for-ever shall be, God's

Chorus
wonderful grace is sufficient for thee, God's grace is
sufficient for me, God's wonderful grace is sufficient for me,
Wherever I may be on land or at sea, God's wonderful grace
is sufficient for me.

NOTES

Chapter 1 Let's Get It Right (Grace)

1   Wallace Henley, *Globequake* (Thomas Nelson Publishers 2012) 99
2   Ibid.
3   Ravi Zacharias, *Cries of the Heart*

Chapter 2 To Be or Not To Be

4   Webster's New Explorer Dictionary and Thesaurus (Merriam-Webster, Inc. 1999) 22
5   Oliver B. Greene, *The Epistle of Paul the Apostle to the Galatians* (The Gospel Inc. 1975) 135
6   Ibid. New Explorer Dictionary 361
7   Ibid. 514
8   Jay R. Leach, *A Light unto My Path* (Trafford Publishers, Inc. 2013) 53
9   David Kinnaman, *You Lost Me* (Baker Books 2011) 99
10 Clark Whitten, *Pure Grace* (Destiny Image Publishers, Inc. 2012) 40

Chapter 3 Living Grace

11 Webster's New Explorer Dictionary and Thesaurus (Merriam-Webster, Inc. 1999) 297

Chapter 4 Graceless Christianity

12 Mike Bickle, *What's Wrong with Grace* (Charisma Media Publication, April, 2013) 32
13 Ibid. 33

Chapter 5 What Kind of People are We (to be?)

14 The NKJV Study Bible notes on Galatians 4 ((Thomas Nelson Publishers 2007) 1851

15 Jay R. Leach, *Behold the Man* (iUniverse Publishing Inc 2011) 61

16 Ibid. 61

17 Ibid. 61

Chapter 6 Living Grace

18 Graham Johnson, *Preaching to a Postmodern World* (Baker Books 2001) 127

19 Andrew Murray, *Humility* (Whitaker House 1982) 10

20 Ibid. 13

21 A.W. Tozer, *The Knowledge of the Holy* (Harper Collins Publishers 1961) 93

22 Graham Johnson, *Preaching to a Postmodern World* (Baker Books 2001) 129

23 Ibid. 130

24 Tozer page 93

Chapter 7 Church and Grace Redefined

25 Rick Warren, *The Purpose Driven Church* (Zondervan Publishing House 1995) 105

26 Jay R. Leach, *Behold the Man* (iUniverse Publishing Inc 2011) 138-139

27 C. Peter Wagner, *Changing Church* (Regal Books 2004) 26

28 Michael Horton, *Putting Amazing Back into Grace* (Baker Book House 2011) 137-139

29 Ibid. 138

30 Charles R. Swindoll, *The Grace Awakening* (Thomas Nelson, Inc.) 9

31 Ibid. 11-12

Chapter 8: A Restored Concept of Ministry

32 Ed Silvoso, *Anointed for Business* (Regal Books 2002) 23

Chapter 9: Intergenerational Dialogue

[33] Jay R. Leach, *How Should We Then Live* (I Universe Publishing Inc. 2010) 65

[34] Accessed 4/19/13 The Barna Group—What Do Americans Really Think About the Bible? http://www.barna.org/culture-articles/609 page 3

[35] Ibid. page 3

[36] Ibid. page 4

[37] Ibid. pages 4-9

[38] Gary L. McIntosh, *One Church Four Generations* (Baker Books 2002) 11

[39] Adapted from, Charles R. Swindoll, *Living on the Raged Edge* (Thomas Nelson Inc. 2004) 93

[40] Accessed from Secular Humanism.org/index.php 10/19/13.

[41] Ibid.

[42] Ibid.

[43] Ibid.

[44] Ibid.

[45] Webster's New Explorer Dictionary and Thesaurus (Merriam-Webster Inc. 1999) 112

[46] Accessed 10/25/13 http://en.wikipedia.org/wiki/william J. Seymour Pages 1-5

[47] The NKJV Study Bible notes on Matthew 16 (Thomas Nelson Publishers 1907) 1516

[48] Ibid. William J. Seymour 1-2

[49] Dr. Bill Hamon, *The Day of the Saints* (Destiny Image, Publishers, Inc. 2002) 180-187

[50] Ibed.184

[51] Ibed.185

[52] Ibed.186

[53] Ibed 187

[54] Ibed 187

[55] Jay R. Leach, *A Light unto My Path* (Trafford Publishing 2013) 88

[56] Ibid. The NKJV Study Bible notes on Romans 8 page 1778

Chapter 10

57 Adapted from Chapter 11, Doctrine of the Atonement: Kevin J. Conner, *The Foundations of Christian Doctrine* (Bible Press, 1980) 203-205
58 Ibid.
59 Ibid.
60 Ibid.
61 Ibid.
62 Adapted from Bruce Wilkinson, *Set Apart* (Multnomah publishers, Inc. 2003) 22

Chapter 11

63 Adapted from Chapter 14, Section IV. The Witness of the Spirit: W.T. Purkiser, Editor, *Exploring Our Christian Faith* (Beacon Hill Press 1978) 285-289